WILD FLOWER

OF AUSTRALIA AND OCEANIA

WILD FLOWERS
OF AUSTRALIA AND OCEANIA

AN ILLUSTRATED GUIDE TO THE FLORAL DIVERSITY OF
AUSTRALIA, NEW ZEALAND AND THE ISLANDS OF THE
PACIFIC OCEAN, WITH 255 PLANT SPECIES AND 625
BOTANICAL ILLUSTRATIONS, MAPS AND PHOTOGRAPHS

MICHAEL LAVELLE

southwater

This edition is published by Southwater
an imprint of Anness Publishing Ltd
Hermes House, 88–89 Blackfriars Road
London SE1 8HA; tel. 020 7401 2077; fax 020 7633 9499

www.southwaterbooks.com; www.annesspublishing.com

If you like the images in this book and would like to
investigate using them for publishing, promotions or
advertising, please visit our website
www.practicalpictures.com for more information.

UK agent: The Manning Partnership Ltd
tel. 01225 478444; fax 01225 478440
sales@manning-partnership.co.uk

UK distributor: Grantham Book Services Ltd
tel. 01476 541080; fax 01476 541061
orders@gbs.tbs-ltd.co.uk

North American agent/distributor: National Book Network
tel. 301 459 3366; fax 301 429 5746; www.nbnbooks.com

Australian agent/distributor: Pan Macmillan Australia
tel. 1300 135 113; fax 1300 135 103
customer.service@macmillan.com.au

New Zealand agent/distributor: David Bateman Ltd
tel. (09) 415 7664; fax (09) 415 8892

Publisher: Joanna Lorenz
Editorial Director: Helen Sudell
Editor: Simona Hill
Illustrators: Anthony Duke, Peter Barrett, Penny Brown
    and Stuart Jackson-Carter
Photographers: Peter Anderson and Geoffrey Brown
Production Controller: Steve Lang

© Anness Publishing Ltd 2008

A CIP catalogue record for this book is available from the
British Library.

Previously published as part of a larger volume, *The
World Encyclopedia of Wild Flowers and Flora*

ETHICAL TRADING POLICY
Because of our ongoing ecological investment
programme, you, as our customer, can have the pleasure
and reassurance of knowing that a tree is being cultivated
on your behalf to naturally replace the materials used to
make the book you are holding. For further information
go to www.annesspublishing.com/trees

CONTENTS

WHAT IS A WILD FLOWER?

The question of what a wild flower is seems steeped in controversy. Purists argue that they must be native to that area, and conservationists often demonize introduced species, despite their having become naturalized and essentially "growing wild".

Flowers are generally considered to be "wild" if they grow without someone having planned where they should be planted. We think of wild flowers as growing in their natural state, with no interference from us, but if we consider the wild species that spring up in gardens, backyards, streets and fields the picture becomes more complex. These plants are indeed wild but thrive in habitats created by humans. In fact, despite every attempt to interfere with their growth, they may well continue to plague farmers, gardeners and city maintenance teams.

Wild flowers are plant species that are at home in a particular place, whether their habitat is natural or the result of human intervention. In any location, from high mountain pastures to great forests, some plants will prosper and others do less well. Each pretty wild flower is the result of countless generations of plants that have striven to exist against staggering odds to ensure that their evolutionary "line" will survive into the future. Some flowers have become highly adapted in order to grow

Above: Traditional heathlands are home to many species of wild flower and flora.

in these places. They may be dependent not only upon their surroundings but upon other plants, for example by providing shelter from weather, or a stem to scramble through; and even dependent upon animals for their survival, for example, to help spread seed or promote root growth by grazing. Many strange and wonderful plant species have been shaped by their homes, their weather and other inhabitants of their habitat into the perfect form for survival.

It is the showiest flowers that we tend to spend most time looking at – how easily we walk past myriad delicate wild flowers to gaze at one large bloom. Every time we walk across a grassy patch we may carelessly crush hundreds of flowering plants

Left: Plants of deciduous woodland, like these bluebells, grow, flower and set seed before the leaf canopy excludes the light in summer.

Above: Shady banks and overgrown roadsides often harbour a rich variety of species that have disappeared from the surrounding area.

underfoot. They are everywhere and many deserve a closer look. A detailed inspection of even the commonest wayside flower reveals an intricacy and beauty that the work of human hands can rarely approach. Wild flowers are among nature's loveliest gifts: carefree and simple, abundant and serendipitous, they provide an ever-changing panorama of colours, shapes, sizes and textures. It is precisely the informal spontaneity of wild flowers – the random mingling of colours and species, and the way that they change through the seasons – that delights us.

The natural floral jewellery that adorns so much of the Earth's surface has enraptured scientists, artists and writers throughout our history, yet it is easy to forget the true depth of this bounty. Its richness is what this book is all about. All flowering plants – even the tiniest ones – deserve our attention, and to understand them fully we must look both closely and carefully. Describing the wonders of just one flower could fill a whole book; to attempt to include here all the flowering plants in Australia and

Oceania would be impossible. This book aims to present a selection: it could be described as a "look through the keyhole" at a world more beautiful than can easily be comprehended. Many plants have had to be omitted and perhaps some of your own favourites are missing. Hopefully, however, you will be inspired to go out and take a fresh look at wild flowers and marvel over these truly remarkable phenomena growing all around us.

Below: Kangaroo paws proliferate in peat-filled swampy ground. Cultivated varieties are available.

HOW FLOWERS LIVE

Flowering plants are the most diverse and widely studied group in the plant kingdom. They are found all across the Earth's surface, wherever plants have learned to live. From mountaintops and the high Arctic to lush tropical forests, flowers are a familiar feature of every landscape. This wide range of habitats has led to flowers assuming a huge diversity of form. In some cases, the flowers have become so reduced as to be insignificant when compared to the plant as a whole. In others, however, the plant itself may hardly be noticed until it produces a huge flower that seems to arrive from nowhere.

Flowers have even driven the process of evolution, harnessing an army of helpers that include almost every conceivable form of land or air living creatures to help with every phase of their reproductive cycle. Many of the showiest flower types trade rich, nutritious, sugary nectar in return for the services of the "diner" in cross fertilization. Flowers are the courtship vessels of plants and are often highly adapted to receive the attention of just a few creatures, some of which are adapted solely to exploit the food source. Others use a variety of tricks and even entrapments to fulfil this need and yet others have abandoned the need for animals, preferring the wind to do the job for them.

Even once the seed is fertilized, the relationship of many species with animals does not end. There are a whole range of ingenious methods by which they recruit animals into spreading their seed for them, and by doing this they not only guarantee the survival of future generations but may also spread the offspring far and wide from the parent plants.

Left: The vivid colours of wild flowers are designed to attract pollinators but have also long attracted the attention of humans.

HOW PLANTS ARE CLASSIFIED

In an attempt to understand the world, humans have become fascinated with the classification of every aspect of it. While such classifications are useful to us, they do not naturally occur in nature and are at best approximations of the true nature of diversity.

Classification helps us to recognize millions of individual species of plants. In pre-literate times plant recognition was a practical necessity, since eating the wrong plants could be fatal.

The earliest written record of a system of plant classification can be attributed to Theophrastus (*c.*372–287BC), a student of Plato and Aristotle, to whom even Alexander the Great sent plant material that he encountered on his expeditions. In his *Enquiry into Plants* and *On the Causes of Plants*, Theophrastus included the classification of species into trees, shrubs, subshrubs and herbs, listing about 500 different plants; he also made a distinction between flowering and non-flowering plants.

The binomial system

The shift toward modern systems of classification began at the time of the Renaissance in Europe (1300–1600). Improvements in navigation, which opened up the world and enabled plants to be collected from much further afield, coincided with the invention of the printing press, which meant information about the new

discoveries could be published widely. Interest in plants increased enormously, and by the 17th century the number of known species was becoming too high to manage without a classification system. The British naturalist John Ray is credited with revising the concept of naming and describing organisms. However, most were classified using a whole string of words that resembled a sentence rather than a name. During the 18th century, the Swedish botanist Carl von Linné (1707–78), who published his work under the Latinized form of his name, Carolus Linnaeus, created a referable system of nomenclature that became the foundation of the system used today. He is often cited as the father of modern taxonomy, or hierarchical classification.

Linnaeus chose to use Latin, then the international language of learned scholars, which enabled scientists speaking and writing different native languages to communicate clearly. His system is now known as binomial

Below: Primula vulgaris, the primrose, gets its genus (first) name from the Latin primus referring to its early appearance in spring.

Above: The rose has been highly bred, and many of the types now in cultivation bear little resemblance to wild types. The genus name, Rosa, is the original Latin name for the plant.

nomenclature (from *bi* meaning "two", *nomen* meaning "name" and *calatus* meaning "called"). Each species is given a generic name – something like a surname – and a specific name, the equivalent of a personal or first name. We still use this system, which has been standardized over the years, for naming and classifying organisms.

The generic (genus) name comes first, and always starts with a capital letter. It is followed by the specific (species) name, which is always in lower case. This combination of genus and species gives a name that is unique to a particular organism. For example, although there are many types of rose in the genus *Rosa*, there is only one called *R. rubiginosa* – commonly known as the sweet briar. (These names are italicized in print.)

The names of plants sometimes change. Name changes usually indicate reclassification of plant species, often as a result of advances in molecular biology. For example, the

Chrysanthemum genus has recently been split into eight different genera, including *Dendranthema*, *Tanacetum* and *Leucanthemum*. It may take the botanical literature years to reflect such changes, and in the meantime inconsistencies in the printed names of plants can appear.

Plant families

Another useful way of classifying plants is by family. Many families are distinctive in terms of their growth characteristics and preferences, while others are very large and diverse, including numerous different genera. There are 380 families of flowering plants, containing all the species known to science that have already been classified. The largest family is the Asteraceae (aster family), which contains 1,317 genera and 21,000 species. In contrast, some plant families are very small: an example is the Cephalotaceae, or saxifragales family, of which a single species, *Cephalotus follicularis*, is found growing along a small stretch of coast in western Australia.

As our understanding increases, and more species are discovered and classified, there is sure to be intense debate over the placement of new and existing species within families.

Below: Geranium (shown here) is often confused with the closely related genus Pelargonium due to Linnaeus (mistakenly) classifying both as Geranium in 1753.

Above: Ferns and mosses represent an ancient lineage of plants that do not produce flowers or seed and as such, are classified as lower plants.

Below: Salad burnet (Sanguisorba minor) is a small herbaceous plant in Rosaceae, yet at first glance it does not appear even remotely similar to the woody genus Rosa.

THE ORIGIN OF SPECIES

The earliest flowering plants appeared on Earth around 350 million years ago in the ancient carboniferous forests, although they really began their "takeover" of the planet 120 million years ago, when the dinosaurs ruled the world.

The first flowers were probably quite insignificant by current standards, but their appearance, coupled with their ability to produce a protective fruit around the seed, marked the beginning of a new era. Despite their rather low key entrance in the early Cretaceous period, by the time the dinosaurs met their end some 55 million years later, most of the major flowering plant groups had already appeared.

Two distinct ways of life emerged for flowering plants. Some continued to reproduce as they had always done – letting the wind control whether pollen from one flower met another flower of the same type. Others, however worked in harmony with insects and other animals, which they enticed with sweet nectar and large, colourful flowers. The relationship was very successful and led to the almost infinite variety of forms and colours that we see around us in plants today.

Below: 500 million years ago non-vascular plants such as hornworts, liverworts, lichens, and mosses grew on Earth.

The first living things

The Earth is around 4.5 billion years old, and life is estimated to have begun around 3.75 billion years ago: for around 750 million years the Earth was (as far as we know) lifeless. It was a hostile environment, with a surface hot enough to boil water and an atmosphere that would have been poisonous to us, yet life is likely to have begun as soon as the surface was cool enough for water to lie on its surface. It was not life as we know it – more a thick soup of chemicals than the miracle of creation – but it was life. This was the situation for 500 million years, until a strange twist of fate assured the rise of the plants.

Primitive single-celled bacteria, which we now know as cyanobacteria, evolved from the existing life forms. They probably appeared remarkably similar to their counterparts, but with one spectacular difference. These cells

Below: 425 million years ago seedless vascular plants such as club mosses, early ferns and horsetails became evident.

were able to take carbon dioxide (which was then very abundant in the Earth's atmosphere) and water and convert them into sugar (an energy-rich food) and oxygen. The effect would have been barely noticeable at first, but over a period of a few hundred million years it changed the atmosphere from one rich in carbon dioxide to one that was at one point almost one-third oxygen. Over this time many of the formerly dominant species died out, but the plant-like bacteria gained the ascendance.

Despite this, plants remained water-bound for another 2.5 billion years. It was not until 425–500 million years ago (a date that is still hotly contested) that they made their first tentative appearance on land. The earliest forms were very simple in comparison to modern plants, but their descendants still exist and probably look similar in many respects – mosses and liverworts

Below: 200 million years ago seeded vascular plants such as the gymnosperms, seed ferns, conifers, cycads and ginkgoes thrived.

are the best examples. The first advance that we know of was marked by the appearance of a plant called *Cooksonia*, 430 million years ago. Within 70 million years, species had diversified and evolved to form lush tropical forests; despite being relatively new to the land, plants had made up for lost time in spectacular style.

The fossil record

Evidence of early plants has been found in the fossil record. As mud and other sediments were deposited, forming rocks, pieces of living organisms were deposited with them. Surviving as fossils, these give us an extraordinary picture of what the Earth was like at any one time. In addition, the chemistry of the atmosphere and hydrosphere (the oceans, rivers, lakes and clouds) of the time can be determined by analysis of the rock. These signs allow us to piece together the story and understand how plants have changed over time.

Darwin's theory of evolution

In 1859, the British naturalist Charles Darwin published *On the Origin of Species*. The work caused a stir at the

Below: 120 million years ago recognizable species of seeded vascular plants, such as magnolias and water lilies evolved.

time as it opposed conventional Church doctrine. Darwin argued that the Earth had been created not tens of thousands of years ago (as the Church claimed) but billions of years ago. The idea was seen as revolutionary or even heretical, but in fact it reflected a growing school of thought that recognized that animal and plant species could change over time. Darwin's grandfather had written on the topic, and Darwin himself acknowledged 20 predecessors who had added to the subject. His original contribution, however, was to sift through this increasing body of evidence and combine it with his own observations during his travels around the world from 1831 to 1836.

Darwin determined that single species, through environmental influence, were able to change over time to suit their surroundings. These changes happened not within the lifetime of an individual organism but through the inheritance of characteristics that were valuable in aiding survival and competing with other organisms for the essentials of life. Though he did not then understand the mechanism by which this happened, Darwin concluded that all modern species have evolved through the process of natural

Above: Though it is a modern species, this Magnolia *flower is very similar to the earliest flower forms of 120 million years ago.*

selection, or "survival of the fittest". The theory revolutionized the study of biology and his work remains a cornerstone of evolutionary science.

Since Darwin's time, the body of evidence has grown. There is still much that we do not know, but many evolutionary scientists believe that there are more species on the planet today than at any time in its entire history. We now mostly understand how changes are passed on to offspring and have been able to piece together an evolutionary hierarchy, where we can see when plants first appeared and how they have changed over time.

Below: Today there are more species of flowering plants in the world than there ever have been at any other time.

THE PARTS OF A PLANT

While plants have undergone many individual changes over millions of years, most of them still have features in common. Flowering plants generally possess roots, stems, leaves and, of course, flowers, all of which may be useful in identifying them.

Learning to recognize species is essentially a question of simple observation combined with knowledge of plant structure. This is because all modern flowering plants have evolved

from a common ancestry – just as most mammals, birds and reptiles possess one head, four limbs, up to five toes per leg and sometimes a tail, because they are all variants of a prior design.

Even when plants have become highly specialized, the common features still persist, albeit in a modified form, and this often betrays a relationship between species that appear unrelated.

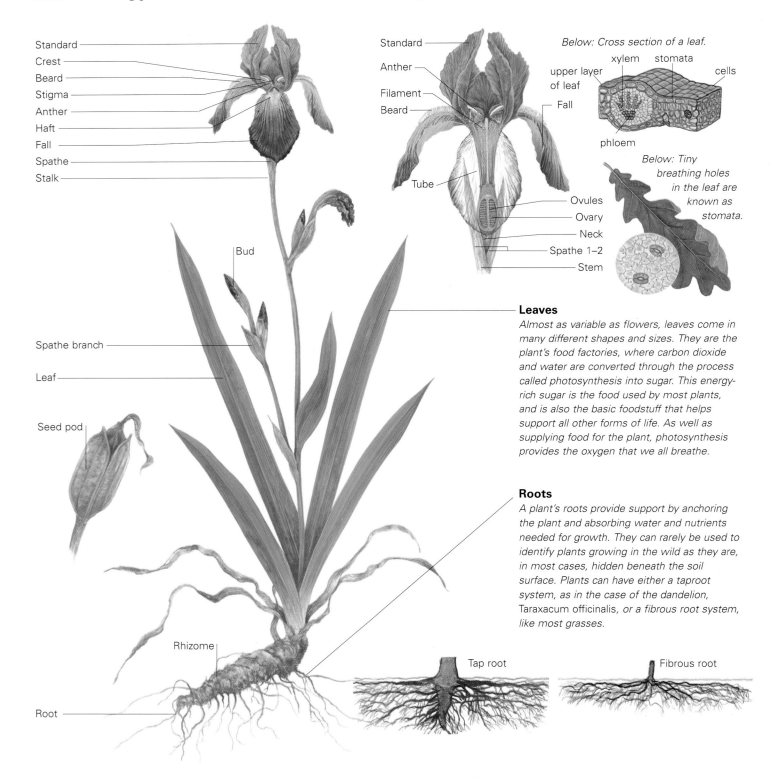

Standard
Crest
Beard
Stigma
Anther
Haft
Fall
Spathe
Stalk

Standard
Anther
Filament
Beard
Fall
Tube
Ovules
Ovary
Neck
Spathe 1–2
Stem

Below: Cross section of a leaf.

xylem   stomata
upper layer of leaf   cells
phloem

Below: Tiny breathing holes in the leaf are known as stomata.

Bud
Spathe branch
Leaf
Seed pod
Rhizome
Root

Tap root   Fibrous root

Leaves

Almost as variable as flowers, leaves come in many different shapes and sizes. They are the plant's food factories, where carbon dioxide and water are converted through the process called photosynthesis into sugar. This energy-rich sugar is the food used by most plants, and is also the basic foodstuff that helps support all other forms of life. As well as supplying food for the plant, photosynthesis provides the oxygen that we all breathe.

Roots

A plant's roots provide support by anchoring the plant and absorbing water and nutrients needed for growth. They can rarely be used to identify plants growing in the wild as they are, in most cases, hidden beneath the soil surface. Plants can have either a taproot system, as in the case of the dandelion, Taraxacum officinalis, or a fibrous root system, like most grasses.

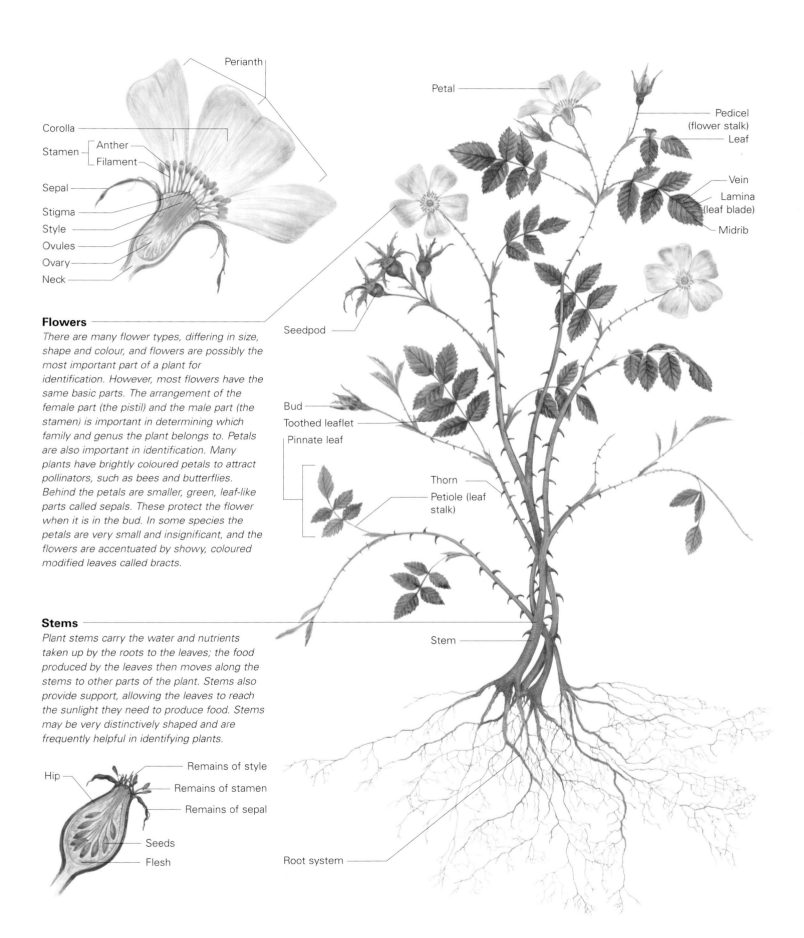

Perianth

Corolla

Stamen — [Anther
[Filament

Sepal

Stigma

Style

Ovules

Ovary

Neck

Petal

Pedicel
(flower stalk)

Leaf

Vein

Lamina
(leaf blade)

Midrib

Seedpod

Bud

Toothed leaflet

Pinnate leaf

Thorn

Petiole (leaf
stalk)

Stem

Flowers

There are many flower types, differing in size, shape and colour, and flowers are possibly the most important part of a plant for identification. However, most flowers have the same basic parts. The arrangement of the female part (the pistil) and the male part (the stamen) is important in determining which family and genus the plant belongs to. Petals are also important in identification. Many plants have brightly coloured petals to attract pollinators, such as bees and butterflies. Behind the petals are smaller, green, leaf-like parts called sepals. These protect the flower when it is in the bud. In some species the petals are very small and insignificant, and the flowers are accentuated by showy, coloured modified leaves called bracts.

Stems

Plant stems carry the water and nutrients taken up by the roots to the leaves; the food produced by the leaves then moves along the stems to other parts of the plant. Stems also provide support, allowing the leaves to reach the sunlight they need to produce food. Stems may be very distinctively shaped and are frequently helpful in identifying plants.

Hip

Remains of style

Remains of stamen

Remains of sepal

Seeds

Flesh

Root system

LEAF FORMS AND SHAPES

While leaves vary considerably in appearance, all are basically similar in terms of their internal anatomy. Leaves are the factories within which plants produce their own food, although in some plants, they have become highly adapted and may fulfil a variety of other roles.

Leaves are able to breathe: air passes freely in and out through specialized pores known as stomata, which are usually found on the lower leaf surface, or epidermis. The stomata can be opened and closed by the plant to regulate water evaporation. This is crucial as it allows the plant to cool down, preventing damage through overheating, though the leaves of some plants (those in dry climates) have few stomata in order to conserve water. Leaves also contain vascular tissue, which is responsible for transporting water to the leaves and food from the leaf to other parts of the plant. The veins are easily visible on both the surface and the underside of most leaves. The same types of tissue are present in the plant's stems and collectively they form a continuous link from root tip to leaf tip.

Leaf fall
When leaves have finished their useful life the plant sheds them. Deciduous trees and shrubs shed all their leaves annually and enter a dormant phase, usually in the autumn in temperate areas or immediately preceding a dry season in warmer climates, to avoid seasonal stresses such as cold or excessive heat damage. Herbaceous

Leaf arrangements
How leaves are attached or arranged on a stem can be a useful tool in plant identification.

Above: Cacti live in very harsh dry conditions and have leaves that are reduced to small spiny pads.

plants (also known as herbs) and other non-woody plants normally lose all of their top growth, including the leaves, for similar reasons. Many plants of the arctic, temperate and dry regions fall into this category.

Plants that do not shed all their leaves at once are said to be evergreen. These plants ride out harsh conditions but may also enter a dormant phase where no new growth commences until conditions improve. Evergreen plants also shed leaves, but tend to do so all through the year, particularly during active growth periods. Many tropical plants fit into this category.

Leaf modifications
Leaves are arguably the most highly modified of all plant organs, and show a vast diversity of form and function. Flower petals are thought to have arisen from leaves. The adaptations in leaves often reflect ways in which

plants have changed in order to cope with specific environmental factors in their natural habitats.

Cactus spines are an example of an extreme leaf modification. The spines are part of a modified leaf called an areole. They are in fact modified leaf hairs, and the small furry base of the spine, or spine cluster, is all that remains of the leaf itself. Cacti and some other succulents have altered so that the stem is the main site of food production, and the leaves have adopted a defensive role.

Other leaf modifications include the development of tendrils to help plants climb, coloured bracts around flowers to attract potential pollinators, and – the most celebrated – traps that attract and ensnare insects to supplement the plant's mineral requirements.

Leaf shape
Leaves grow in a tremendous variety of sizes and shapes, which can be useful in helping to identify the plant.
• Leaf margins, or edges, occur in a variety of forms. The simplest is a smooth, continuous line, which is described as "entire". Often, however, the edge is broken up in a definite pattern, such as "serrated" or "lobed".
• The apex, or leaf tip, may vary in shape, even between closely related species. This may reflect environmental factors. The base of the leaf is also variable and is considered along with the way the leaf is attached to the stem.
• Veination may form an identifiable trait. Monocotyledonous plants have parallel veins that run the length of the leaf. Dicotyledonous plants have a netted arrangement that is complex.
• Leaves can be categorized as simple or compound. A simple leaf is one single leaf blade on a stalk. Compound leaves are made up of a group of leaflets, with a single stalk, attaching the group to the stem.

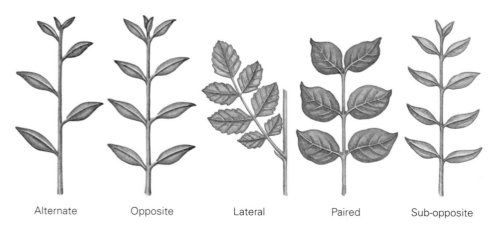

Alternate   Opposite   Lateral   Paired   Sub-opposite

Leaf shapes

Leaves are almost as varied as flowers in respect of their shapes, although they offer less of a clue as to the relationships between even quite closely related species. Similar shapes, sizes and colours of leaf may occur on quite unrelated species and it is thought that this is mainly due to the original environmental circumstances that a plant evolved within.

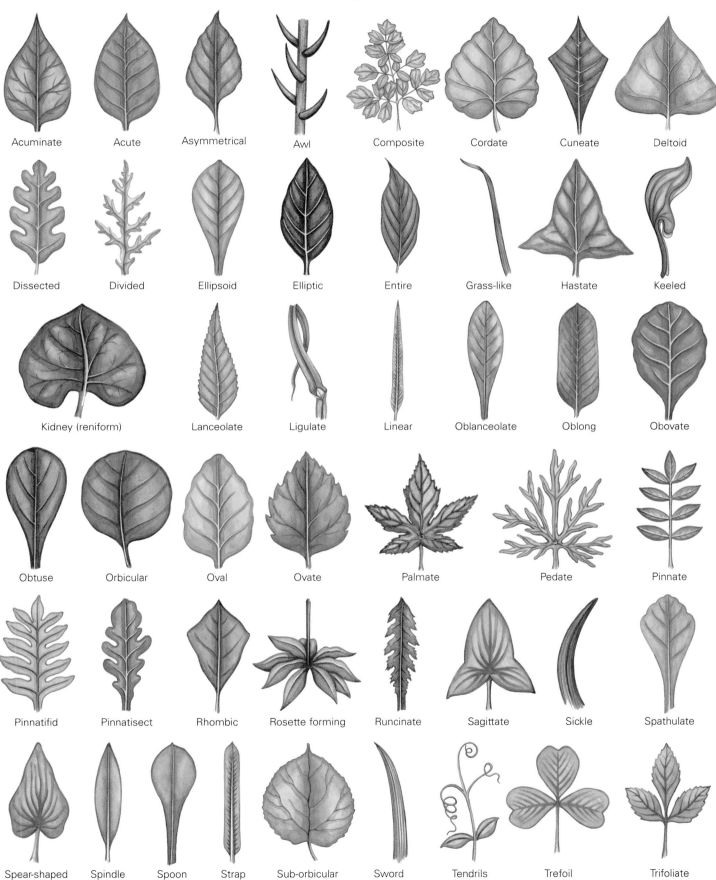

Acuminate   Acute   Asymmetrical   Awl   Composite   Cordate   Cuneate   Deltoid

Dissected   Divided   Ellipsoid   Elliptic   Entire   Grass-like   Hastate   Keeled

Kidney (reniform)   Lanceolate   Ligulate   Linear   Oblanceolate   Oblong   Obovate

Obtuse   Orbicular   Oval   Ovate   Palmate   Pedate   Pinnate

Pinnatifid   Pinnatisect   Rhombic   Rosette forming   Runcinate   Sagittate   Sickle   Spathulate

Spear-shaped   Spindle   Spoon   Strap   Sub-orbicular   Sword   Tendrils   Trefoil   Trifoliate

FLOWERS AND FLOWER FORMS

A flower is the reproductive organ of plants classified as angiosperms – plants that flower and form fruits containing seeds. The function of a flower is to produce seeds through sexual reproduction. The seeds produce the next generation of a species and are the means by which the species is able to spread.

It is generally thought that a flower is the product of a modified stem, with the petals being modified leaves. The flower stem, called a pedicel, bears on its end the part of the flower called the receptacle. The various other parts are arranged in whorls on the receptacle: four main whorls make up a flower.

• The outermost whorl, located nearest the base of the receptacle where it joins the pedicel, is the calyx. This is made up of sepals (modified leaves that typically enclose the closed flower bud), which are usually green but may appear very like petals in some flowers, such as narcissus.

• The next whorl is the corolla – more commonly known as the petals. These are usually thin, soft and coloured, and are used to attract pollinators such as insects.

• The androecium (from the Greek *andros* and *oikia*, meaning "man's house") contains the male flower parts, consisting of one or two whorls of stamens. Each stamen consists of a filament topped by an anther, where pollen is produced.

• The last and innermost whorl is the gynoecium (from the Greek *gynaikos*

Flower shapes
Flowers display a wide variety of shapes that may be the result of individual flowers or the close arrangement into a flower-like compound inflorescence.

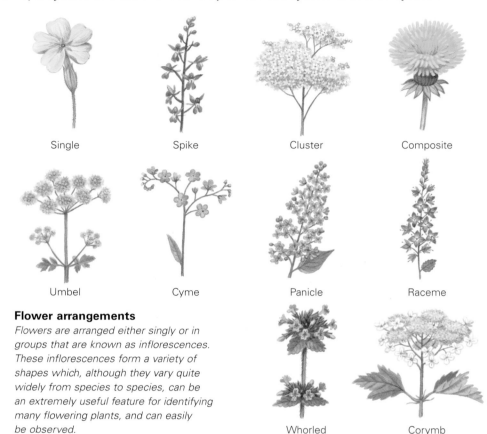

Single   Spike   Cluster   Composite

Umbel   Cyme   Panicle   Raceme

Whorled   Corymb

Flower arrangements
Flowers are arranged either singly or in groups that are known as inflorescences. These inflorescences form a variety of shapes which, although they vary quite widely from species to species, can be an extremely useful feature for identifying many flowering plants, and can easily be observed.

and *oikia*, meaning "woman's house"), which consists of a pistil with one or more carpels. The carpel is the female reproductive organ, containing an ovary with ovules. The sticky tip of the pistil – the stigma – is where pollen must be deposited in order to fertilize the seed. The stalk that supports this is known as the style.

This floral structure is considered typical, though many plant species show a wide variety of modifications from it. However, despite the differences between genera, most flowers are simply variations on a theme and a basic knowledge of their arrangement is all you really need to get started with their identification.

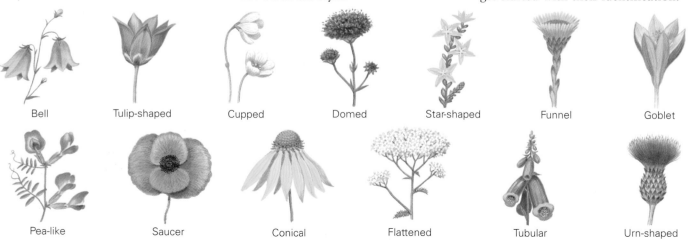

Bell   Tulip-shaped   Cupped   Domed   Star-shaped   Funnel   Goblet

Pea-like   Saucer   Conical   Flattened   Tubular   Urn-shaped

Monoecious and dioecious plants

In most species, the individual flowers have both a pistil and several stamens, and are described by botanists as "perfect" (bisexual or hermaphrodite). In some species, however, the flowers are "imperfect" (unisexual) and possess either male or female parts only. If each individual plant has either only male or only female flowers, the species is described as dioecious (from the Greek *di* and *oikia*, meaning "two houses"). If unisexual male and female flowers both appear on the same plant, the species is described as monoecious (from the Greek *mono* and *oikia*, meaning "one house").

Attracting pollinators

Many flowers have evolved specifically to attract animals that will pollinate them and aid seed formation. These commonly have nectaries – specialized glands that produce sugary nectar – in order to attract such animals. As many

Different growing habits

Plants exhibit a variety of growing habits, often reflecting the type of habitat or niche they have specifically evolved to occupy. These are often important features to note when identifying a plant as the flowers may not be present all year round. The growing habits shown below describe all of the flowers that are featured in this directory.

Above: Flowers that attract bees will often have petals that form a wide surface for landing and copious amounts of nectar.

pollinators have colour vision, brightly coloured flowers have evolved to attract them. Flowers may also attract pollinators by scent, which is often attractive to humans – though not always: the flower of the tropical rafflesia, for example, which is pollinated by flies, produces a smell like that of rotting flesh.

There are certain flowers whose form is so breathtaking as to render them almost unnatural to our eyes. Flowering plants such as orchids have developed a stunning array of forms and many have developed intricate relationships with their pollinators. Flowers that are pollinated by the wind have no need to attract animals and therefore tend not to be showy.

Above: Flowers whose petals form a protective cup or tube are especially attractive to butterflies or other insects with long mouthparts.

Types of inflorescence

Some plants bear only one flower per stem, called solitary flowers. Many other plants bear clusters of flowers, which are known as inflorescences. Most inflorescences may be classified into two groups, racemes and cymes.

In a raceme, the individual flowers making up the inflorescence bloom progressively from the bottom of the stem to the top. Racemose inflorescences include arrangements called spike, raceme, corymb, umbel and head. In the cyme group, the top floret opens first and the blooms continue to open downward along the peduncle, or inflorescence stalk. Cymes may be simple or compound.

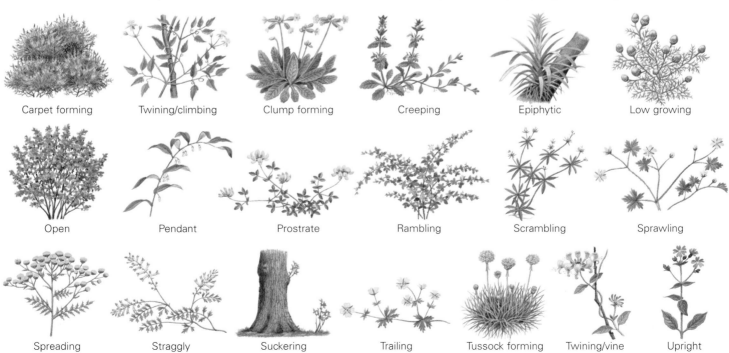

Carpet forming | Twining/climbing | Clump forming | Creeping | Epiphytic | Low growing

Open | Pendant | Prostrate | Rambling | Scrambling | Sprawling

Spreading | Straggly | Suckering | Trailing | Tussock forming | Twining/vine | Upright

THE LIFE CYCLE OF FLOWERING PLANTS

All flowering plants, from giant forest trees that live for thousands of years to the most ephemeral desert annuals that live for only a few weeks, follow the same pattern of life. Their lifespan, size, apparent durability and survival strategies vary considerably, but they have much in common.

Above: Field poppy, Papaver rhoeas, *is an annual that completes its life cycle in one season.*

Above: Wild carrot, Daucus carota, *is a biennial that grows one year and flowers the next.*

Above: Yellow flag, Iris pseudacorus, *is a perennial that lives and flowers for many years.*

All flowering plants begin life as seeds. These are in essence tiny, baby plants that have been left in a state of suspended animation with enough food to support them in the first few days of their new life. In order to grow, seed must be viable (alive). It is a misconception that seed is not living. It is and, like all living things, has a lifespan. However, many types of seed can remain dormant for decades, waiting for the right opportunity to commence their cycle of growth and development.

Eventually, the seed will be triggered into germinating by the right combination of moisture, temperature and a suitable soil or growing medium.

Some seeds have specific needs; proteas and banksias must be exposed to smoke to prompt germination, and many berries, such as mistletoe, need to be exposed to the stomach acid of an animal. In most cases, the germinating plant is totally reliant on the energy stored in the seed until it pushes its growing tip above the soil.

The maturing plant

Once above ground the stem grows up toward the light and soon produces leaves that unfold and begin to harvest light energy. As the stems grow upward the plant also extends its roots down into the soil, providing stability and allowing the plant to harvest both water and minerals that are vital to its growth.

Once the plant reaches its mature phase of growth, changes in its internal chemistry enable it to begin flowering. When this happens depends upon the species, but many plants – except those with the briefest life cycles – continue to grow while they produce flower buds. These buds develop into flowers, which are pollinated by the wind or by pollinators such as bees, moths or other animals.

Once a flower has been pollinated, it will usually fade quickly before turning into fruit, as the fertilized

Yearly life cycle of herbaceous plants

All flowering plants begin life as a seed. Some grow and flower within the first season, while others grow for several years before they flower. Herbaceous plants whether annual or perennial, grow and flower before dying back down at the end of the season.

ovary swells and the new seeds develop. The seeds will continue to develop within the fruit until the embryos are fully mature and the seeds are capable of growing into new plants. This may be very quick in the case of small herbs, but in some shrubs and trees it can take two or more seasons for the seeds to develop fully.

Plants may take just one season to reach flowering stage, or may live for many years before they flower. Once flowering begins, certain species flower repeatedly for many seasons, some lasting decades or even centuries. There is much variability between species, but most plants follow one of three main types of life cycle.

Annuals

Plants that live for a single growing season, or less, are called annuals. Their life cycle is completed within a year. In this time the plant will grow, flower, set fruit containing seeds, and die. Many common flowering plants adopt this strategy which has the advantage of allowing them to colonize areas quickly and make the best of the available growing conditions.

Biennials

Plants that need two growing seasons to complete their life cycle are known as biennials. Generally, biennials germinate and grow foliage in the first growing season before resting over the

winter. In the second growing season the plant enters a mature phase, in which it flowers, sets fruit and then dies. A biennial flowers only once before dying. A few plants may grow only foliage for several years before finally flowering and dying.

Perennials

All the remaining plant types live for three or more years, and may go on growing, flowering and producing fruit for many years. Some perennial species may take a number of years to grow to flowering size, but all of them are characterized by a more permanent existence than that of annuals and biennials.

Life cycle of a dandelion

Above: The flower begins life as a tight bud that opens from the tip to reveal the yellow petals of the tiny individual flowers.

Above: As the flower opens further, it widens and flattens in order to make a perch for the bumblebees, which are its pollinators.

Above: Once the flower has been pollinated, it closes up again and the plant commences the process of seed production.

Above: Once the seed is ripened, the flower bracts re-open, and the parachute-like seed appendages (achenes) spread to form a globe.

Above: As the ripened seed dries, it is easily dislodged and is carried away from the parent plant by even a light breeze.

Above: Once the seed has been dispersed, the flower stalk is redundant and quickly withers, leaving only the leafy rosette.

WHAT IS POLLINATION?

Before a flower can develop seeds for reproduction it must be pollinated: pollen must be moved from the male anthers to the female stigma. There are many ways that flowers can be pollinated, but each species is designed to be pollinated in a specific way.

Some flowers are able to self-pollinate – when pollen from their own anthers is deposited on the stigma – but for most, pollination needs some outside help. Wind moves the pollen for some plants, of which grasses are a prime example, but others require the assistance of an animal pollinator. These move pollen from the anthers to the stigma of a flower, and also often carry it between different flowers or plants of the same species. Many animals are known to be good pollinators but those that most commonly perform this task include bees, butterflies, hummingbirds, moths, some flies, some wasps and nectar-feeding bats.

The benefits of pollination

Plants benefit from pollinators because the movement of pollen allows them to set seed and ultimately begin a new generation. The pollinators, however, are not acting for the benefit of the plant. For them, pollination is an incidental by-product of their efforts to collect nectar and/or pollen from flowers for themselves or their own offspring. In evolutionary terms it is a perfect example of two unrelated species gradually adapting to mutual dependence, where both benefit from

Below: Pollinators, such as this swallowtail butterfly, feed upon the energy- and protein-rich nectar while pollinating the plant.

the relationship. Indeed, many plants have become so dependent on a particular pollinator that their flowers have become specifically adapted to favour them. The loss of the pollinating animal from a habitat may ultimately result in the extinction of the plant as well.

Fertilization

Once a pollen grain has landed on the stigma, it must reach the ovaries of the flower in order to fuse with the female cell and begin to form a seed. It does this by germinating and growing a long thin tube that reaches down the style into the flower's ovaries. The pollen tube provides a pathway for the male chromosomes to reach the egg cell in the ovule. One pollen grain fertilizes one egg cell, and together they form the new seed.

Flower forms and pollinators

Plants that are wind-pollinated often have flowers that are small, numerous and inconspicuous. They produce huge amounts of pollen, which saturates the air around them to ensure that some reaches nearby plants.

Plants pollinated by bees usually have yellow or blue flowers that are sweetly fragrant and produce sweet nectar. Bees tend to visit flowers whose petals form a wide enough surface for them to land upon. As they take the nectar the visiting bees are dusted with pollen, which is brushed off on the next flowers they visit.

Some plants are pollinated by beetles. Their flowers are usually white or dull in colour, mostly with yeasty, spicy or fruity odours. They may or may not produce nectar, as pollen is often the source of food that they seek.

Flowers that rely on fly pollination usually possess flowers that are dull red or brown and have foul odours: in some cases this may be accompanied

Fertilization

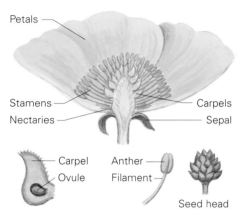

Above: In this buttercup the male flower parts (stamens, each comprised of an anther and a filament) are laden with pollen and surround female parts (carpels) containing ovules (eggs).

Above and below: Bees tend to visit flowers whose petals form a wide enough surface for them to land upon. As they take the nectar the bees are dusted with pollen, which brushes on to the flowers they visit next.

Once a pollen grain has landed on the stigma, it must reach the ovaries of the flower in order to fuse with the female cell and begin to form a seed. It does this by germinating and growing a long thin tube that reaches down the style into the flower's ovaries. The pollen tube provides a pathway for the male chromosomes to reach the egg cell in the ovule. One pollen grain fertilizes one egg cell, and together they form the new seed.

Above: Bees need a flat landing platform on which to rest before collecting pollen from plants.

Above: A common sparrow feeding on Kniphofia *species aids the pollination process as it eats. Like other birds its pointed beak can reach high into tubular flowerheads to collect food.*

by nectar that resembles (in taste and smell) rotting meat.

Butterflies mainly pollinate flowers that are relatively long and tubular in shape – although this can vary considerably – while moths typically pollinate flowers that are yellow or white and fragrant, as they visit them at night.

Some plants are pollinated by birds, though they are far fewer than those visited by insects. Plants that attract hummingbirds, for example, have brightly coloured flowers but very little fragrance, since the birds have no sense of smell. All bird-pollinated flowers are similar in structure to those pollinated by butterflies, in that they have a long tubular shape, but they produce even greater amounts of nectar.

Self-pollination and cross-pollination

While it is possible for some individual plants to pollinate their own flowers, this is not ideal because inbreeding limits them genetically. Many plants have developed some factor that promotes cross-pollination between different individuals of the same species.

Dioecious plants (those with separate male and female plants) achieve cross-pollination by their very nature. No self-pollination is possible

because each plant produces either male or female parts only.

Monoecious plants (those that produce female and male flower parts on the same plant) may avoid self-pollination by having their male and female parts mature at different times. Protandrous flowers produce pollen before the stigma is ripe and ready to receive it. The situation is reversed in the case of protogynous flowers, in which the stigma is ready to receive pollen from other flowers before its stamens ripen and produce their own. In cases where the male and female structures mature at the same time, the physical separation of the stamens and stigma can also help prevent self-pollination. Other species are genetically designed so that pollen from the same flower, or from other flowers on the same plant, cannot cause fertilization. This design – known as self-incompatibility – ensures that seed production results only from cross-pollination with a separate plant.

Right: Grasses have very small, fine and lightweight seeds that are dispersed quickly in the slightest breeze. This method of seed dispersal can carry the seeds far away from the parent plant.

Despite the genetic benefits of cross-pollination, however, self-pollination is the norm in some species. It may be desirable where a given genotype is particularly adapted to an environment. Another advantage is that the species does not have to depend on pollination agents to reproduce.

SEEDS AND SEED DISPERSAL

For flowering plants, seed production is the main method of reproduction. Seeds have the advantage of providing the plants with a way to spread and grow in new places, which in some cases may be at a distance from the parent. Their ability to do this is extremely important.

If seeds were not dispersed the result would be many germinating seedlings growing very close to the parent plant, leading to a crowded mass of the same species. Each of the seedlings would be in direct competition with the others, and with the parent plant, for light, space, water and nutrients. Few of the offspring (or the parent) would prosper from this arrangement.

Seeds are dispersed using a number of different strategies. The majority tend to be carried by wind, water or animals, though some plants have adopted the strategy of shooting seeds out explosively.

Wind dispersal

Seeds that depend upon wind dispersal are usually very light in weight. Orchid seeds, for example, are almost as fine as dust and easily float along in a light breeze. In addition to lightness, composite flowers such as the dandelion, *Taraxacum officinalis*, have hairy appendages on each seed that act like parachutes, carrying the seeds over long distances. In species such as the field poppy, *Papaver rhoeas*, the wind plays a part in dispersal by causing the ripe fruits to sway to and fro, shaking

Above: For plants growing near the water's edge, the water may act to transport the seed far from the parent plant.

out the seeds like pepper from a pepper pot. These seeds are often very light and small and may be carried farther away by the wind.

The small size of wind-dispersed seeds is reflected in the amount of food

reserves stored in them. Larger seeds contain greater food reserves, allowing the young seedlings more time to grow before they must begin manufacturing their own food. The longer a seedling has before it must become self-sufficient, the greater its chance of becoming successfully established. However, large seeds have the disadvantage that they are more difficult to disperse effectively by wind or explosive techniques.

Explosions

Some plants have pods that explode when ripe, shooting out the seeds. Many members of the pea family, Papilionaceae, scatter their seeds in this way. Once the seeds are ripe and the pod has dried, it bursts open and the seeds are scattered. In some of these plants, such as common gorse, *Ulex europaeus*, seed dispersal is further enhanced because the seeds possess a waxy cuticle that ants like to eat, thus encouraging the ants to carry them around. Another explosive technique is used by the Mediterranean

Below: The opium poppy, Papaver somnifera, *releases its seed when shaken by the wind. Because the seed is tiny it can be carried far away from the parent plant. Each seed head produces masses of seed.*

Below: The Mediterranean squirting cucumber, Ecballium elaterium, *releases the seed as part of a liquid mucilage, which is squirted from the plant when the parent reaches maturity.*

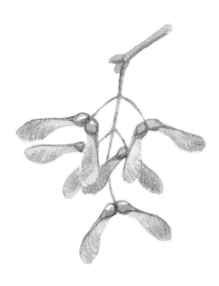

Above: Seeds of the sycamore tree are held in "keys", which float on the wind and disperse the contents far from the parent plant.

Above: Squirrels are well-known collectors of nuts, which they bury in the ground and may never return to collect.

squirting cucumber, *Ecballium elaterium*: it has a fleshy, almost liquid, fruit that, when ripe, squirts its jelly-like contents – along with the seeds – some distance from the plant. The action is visible to the human eye.

Water dispersal

The fruit and seeds of many aquatic or waterside plants are able to float. Water lily seeds, for example, are easily dispersed to new locations when carried by moving water, and coconuts can travel huge distances across seas and oceans, which is why coconut palms grow on so many Pacific islands – the original nuts were carried there on ocean currents from the mainland. Mangroves, which are the dominant vegetation of coastal marshes in the tropics, are another example of plants that disperse their seeds by water.

Animal dispersal

The production of a nutritious, fleshy fruit that animals like to eat is another strategy that many plants have adopted. An animal eating the fruit digests only the fleshy outer part. The well-protected seeds – the stones (pits) or pips in the fruit – pass through the animal's digestive system and are excreted in droppings that provide a

rich growing medium to get the plant started. The seeds are often deposited a long way from the parent plant by this means.

Many types of mistletoe have sticky fruits that are attractive to birds. The sticky berries create equally sticky droppings that the bird needs to "rub off" on the branches of trees. The seeds are deposited, with the droppings, on the bark to grow into new mistletoe plants.

A few plants, such as common burdock, *Arctium pubens*, produce seeds with hooks that catch on the fur of animals and are carried away. The animal eventually removes the burrs through grooming or moulting, and the seeds are then deposited on the ground.

Fire

Some plants living in fire-prone areas have evolved traits that allow them to use this to their advantage when reproducing or regenerating. For most of these species, the intensity of the fire is crucial to seed dispersal: it must be hot, but not so hot that it cooks the seed. In addition, fires should not occur too frequently, as the plant must have time to grow and mature so that new seed can be produced.

Many fire-tolerant species have cones that open only after a fire. Plants using this strategy are described as serotinous. Many plants that grow in

the Australian bush or in the fynbos (the natural vegetation of South Africa's southern Cape region) are very reliant on fire. In many cases the heat triggers seed dispersal but it is the chemical constituents of the smoke that initiate seed germination.

Below: While fire decimates crops and forces wildlife out of the immediate vicinity, the heat generated by fire can trigger germination in some plant species.

HERBACEOUS PLANTS

Looking at plants in the wild, it quickly becomes apparent that there are two basic types. Those that have permanent woody stems, whose shoots do not die back, are generally referred to as trees and shrubs. The remainder lack permanent stems and are often described as herbaceous plants, or herbs.

Herbaceous plants are those that die to the ground each year and produce new stems in the following growing season. The word is used in a broader sense, however, to describe any plant with soft, non-woody tissues, whether it is an annual, perennial or bulb.

To understand how these plants live and grow, we can begin by looking at a seedling. In all seedlings and small plants it is the water content of the cells in the leaves and stems that holds the plants erect. All young plants are similar in this respect but as they grow, woody plants begin to build up the strengthening layers of their characteristic structure. Non-woody plants, on the other hand, always retain soft stems.

Below: Grasslands are an ideal habitat for many herbaceous plants and provide a home for a rich diversity of species.

Above: The water hyacinth, Eichhornia crassipes, *is a non-woody plant that has become adapted to an aquatic lifestyle.*

Stem structure

Soft stems remain upright because their cells have rigid walls, and water in the cells helps retain their shape. This has the obvious disadvantage that during a dry period water can be drawn out of the cells; the cells become limp and the plant droops or wilts. Many species have stems with a soft inner part – commonly called the pith – that is used to store food. Others, however, have hollow cylindrical stems. In these, the vascular bundles (the veins that transport water, nutrients and sugars around the plant) are arranged near the outside of the stem. This cylindrical formation gives the stem a much greater strength than a solid structure of the same weight.

The relatively short lifespan of non-woody plants (compared with that of many woody plants) and the lack of a strong, rigid structure generally limit the height to which they can grow. Despite this, plants such as the giant hogweed, *Heracleum mantegazzianum*, can easily reach heights of 3–4m/10–13ft – larger than many shrubs. Such giants are rare, however, and most herbaceous plants are no more than 1–2m/3–6½ft in height.

Survival strategies

Non-woody plants usually produce completely new stems each year, because cold or other adverse weather (such as drought) causes the stems to die back to the ground. The climate in which the plant grows greatly affects the survival strategy it adopts. Some species survive periods of cold by forming underground bulbs or tubers for food storage, while others – the annuals – complete their life cycles within one growing season, after which the whole plant dies.

Herbaceous plants are generally divided into those with broad leaves (called forbs) and grass-like plants with very narrow leaves (called graminoids). Some species have become herbaceous vines, which climb on other plants. Epiphytes have gone one step further: they germinate and live their whole life on other plants, never coming in contact with the soil. Many orchids and bromeliads are epiphytes. Other species have adapted to life largely submerged in water, becoming aquatic plants. Many of these are rooted in the sediment at the bottom of the water, but a few have adapted to be completely free floating.

Below: Open woodland and forest clearings are often rich in herbaceous plants that enjoy the shelter and light shady conditions.

Right: Bulbs such as this petticoat daffodil, Narcissus bulbocodium, flower in spring in alpine pasture before dying down to avoid the hot dry summer.

A few species have adapted to use the efforts of other plants to their own ends. Some are semi-parasites – green plants that grow attached to other living, green plants. These unusual plants still photosynthesize but also supplement their nutrients by "stealing" them directly from their unfortunate host plants. A few species, however, are wholly parasitic – totally dependent upon their host for nutrition. They do not possess any chlorophyll and are therefore classed as "non-green" plants. Many remain hidden, either inside the host plant or underground, appearing to the outside world only when they produce flowers.

Subshrubs

Some plants, while they are woody in nature, resemble non-woody plants because of their small size coupled with their ability to shoot strongly from ground level or from below ground. They are known as "subshrubs", a term borrowed from horticulture, where it is used to describe any plant that is treated as a herb in respect of its cultivation. In

terms of wild plants it is used rarely to describe low-growing, woody or herbaceous evergreen perennials whose shoots die back periodically.

Small plants

The world's smallest plant species is water meal, *Wolffia globosa*, a floating aquatic herb which, when mature, is not much larger than the full stop at the end of this sentence. Despite its small size, it is a flowering plant. The flowers occur only rarely and would be hard to see without the aid of a microscope. It mainly reproduces vegetatively and quickly forms a large floating colony on the surface of slow-flowing or still water.

WOODY PLANTS

Any vascular plant with a perennial woody stem that supports continued growth above ground from year to year is described as a woody plant. A true woody stem, however, contains wood, which is mainly composed of structured cellulose and lignin.

Cellulose is the primary structural component of plants, and lignin is a chemical compound that is an integral part of the cell walls. Most of the tissue in the woody stem is non-living, and although it is capable of transporting water it is simply the remains of cells that have died. This is because most woody plants form new layers of tissue each year over the layer of the preceding year. They thus increase their stem diameter from year to year and, as each new layer forms, the underlying one dies. So big woody plants are merely a thin living skin stretched over a largely lifeless framework of branches. In effect, as a woody plant grows, the proportion of living material compared to the non-living parts steadily decreases.

Bamboos appear to be woody plants, and indeed do have permanent woody stems above the ground, but are more akin to the grasses, to which they are closely related, than to the commoner woody species. Essentially, they grow a dense stand of individual

Below: Bamboos are the only examples of the grass family to have evolved permanent stems above ground.

Above: All woody plants can be defined by their permanent, often long-lived growth.

stems that emerge from underground stems called rhizomes. In many ways their biology is more like that of non-woody plants, despite their appearance.

Pros and cons of woody stems

There are more than 80,000 species of tree on earth and a considerably higher number of shrubby species. Although the exact number is not known, it is obvious even to a novice plant spotter that woody plants are an extremely successful group. This is because they are bigger than other plants, so they are able to gather more light and therefore produce more food. In areas where inclement weather induces plants to enter a seasonal dormant period, woody plants have the advantage of a head start when growth restarts. They do not have to compete with other emerging plants and can start producing a food from the moment they recommence growth.

Despite their obvious success, however, woody plants have not managed to dominate the entire

land surface. Only the largest trees are fully immune to the effects of large plant-eating mammals, and in some areas, such as the tundra, weather patterns are so extreme that only low-growing woody plants can survive, and they must compete with the surrounding herbage.

Support strategies

As well as trees and large shrubs, there are woody species that exploit other woody plants around them. Lianas, for instance, germinate on the ground and maintain soil contact, but use another plant for support. Many common climbers or vines are lianas.

Somewhat more unusual are the hemi-epiphytes, which also use other plants for support, at least during part of their life: some species germinate on other plants and then establish soil contact, while others germinate on the ground but later lose contact with the soil. The strangler figs, *Ficus* species, are interesting examples: they begin life as epiphytes,

Below: Woody plants include the largest living plant species, the giant redwood Sequoiadendron giganteum, *among their ranks.*

Above: The permanent stems of woody plants are prone to disease, such as this canker, and older specimens contain much deadwood.

Above: Mistletoe is a shrubby plant that has adapted to be partially parasitic on other, larger woody plants such as trees.

Above: Cacti are highly specialized plants that are descended from woody ancestry and have highly specialized permanent stems.

growing on other trees, unlike other tree seedlings that have to start their struggle for survival on the forest floor. The young strangler fig grows slowly at first, as little water or food is available to it, but its leathery leaves reduce water loss. It then puts out long, cable-like roots that descend the trunk of the host tree and root into the soil at its foot. Now readily able to absorb nutrients and water, the young fig tree flourishes. The thin roots thicken and interlace tightly around the supporting tree trunk. The

Below: Evergreen shrubs, such as this Rhododendron ponticum, produce food all year round and may form dense understorey in deciduous woodland.

expanding leafy crown of the strangler shades the crown of the support tree and its roots start to strangle its host. The host tree eventually dies and slowly rots away, leaving a totally independent strangler fig, which may live for several hundred years.

Other woody plants, such as the mistletoe, "plug" themselves into a branch of a living tree and harvest nutrients directly from it. Apart from a free supply of food and water they gain the added advantage of being high above competing plants and trees, so that they receive enough light to photosynthesize. Mistletoe is a partial parasite that retains its woody stems and green leaves.

The largest plants

The identity of the world's largest plant is debatable, not only because woody plants are only partly living tissue, but also because it has still not been fully researched. In practice, it is extremely difficult to measure how much of a tree is actually living tissue, although the usual candidate is the giant redwood, *Sequoiadendron giganteum*. The banyan tree, *Ficus benghalensis*, can easily cover an area of 2 hectares/5 acres, and the related *Ficus religiosa* can allegedly cover even more. Whether any of these species are really the largest is a moot point, but it is certain that the title of largest flowering plant will always be held by a woody species.

The oldest plants

Among the oldest plants on Earth are the bristlecone pines, *Pinus longaeva*. Some individuals are known to be more than 4,000 years old and others are estimated to be 5,000 years old. Some creosote plants, *Larrea divaricata* ssp. *tridentata*, are even older. The creosote plant sends up woody stems directly from ground level, so that all the stems in a dense stand are clones of the original plant. An ancient stand in California's Mojave Desert, known as the King's Clone, is estimated to be 11,700 years old, although the individual stems live for much shorter periods.

ECOLOGY AND HABITATS

The study of the ways in which plants, animals and their environment interact with one another is known as ecology. All evolutionary change takes place as a direct response to the ecological pressures that affect the plants and animals in a particular habitat.

Ecology is a scientific discipline that contributes greatly to our understanding of all living things and of evolution. The pressures that affect plants and animals in any given habitat may be a result of direct interaction between species – for example, plants may be grazed by animals or damaged by insects – or they may be the result of changes in the wider environment, such as the changing seasons or the effect of flooding. Sometimes the effects of these interactions may be noticed across many habitats, on a regional or even global scale.

Interaction

In order to understand the complexities of even relatively small habitats, three basic principles must be remembered. First, living things do not exist as isolated individuals or groups of individuals. They are part of a continuum of life that stretches across the entire surface of the earth. Second, all organisms interact with other

Below: Plants such as the California poppy, Eschscholzia californica, are vulnerable to habitat loss.

members of their own species, with other species, and with their physical and chemical environments. Third, all organisms have an effect on each other and their surroundings, and as they interact with both they may actually change them over time: for example, trees gradually modify the soil they grow in by constantly dropping dead leaves that decompose and are incorporated into it.

Plant groups

The plants within an environment are grouped together in a number of ways.
• A "species" is a natural group of individuals that interbreed, or have the potential to do so, and will not normally interbreed with other related groups.
• A "population" describes all the individuals of a given species in a defined area, such as all the dandelions in an area of grassland.
• A "community" refers to the total grouping of all the different populations that occur together in a particular area.
• An "ecosystem" is the community, or

Above: Grazing animals may change or even destroy habitats where densities of animals become too high.

series of communities, together with the surrounding environment. It includes the physical and chemical environment, such as the rocks, water and air.

In an ecosystem, all the organisms composing the populations and communities require energy for survival. In the case of the plants, that energy comes from the sun: plants use sunlight for photosynthesis, which

Above: Water voles inhabit riverbanks and slow-moving streams and grassland. They are dependent on grasses for their survival.

converts the light energy into basic sugars, which the plant uses as its food and stores in the form of sugars, starches and other plant material. Any animals in the ecosystem derive their energy from this store, either by eating the plants or by eating other animals that feed on the plants.

Habitats

The location where a particular species is normally found is its "habitat". A single ecosystem may contain many different habitats in which organisms can live. Salt marsh ecosystems, for example, include areas that are flooded twice daily by tides as well as areas that are inundated only by the highest tides of the month or the year. Different plants inhabit each of these areas, though there may be some overlap, but they are all considered inhabitants of the same ecosystem. Some plants can thrive and reproduce in several different habitats, as long as each provides the appropriate combination of environmental factors: the correct amount of light, water, the necessary temperature range, nutrients, and a substrate on which to grow: sand, clay, peat, water or even another plant may be appropriate. All these factors must be within the range of the plants' tolerance. Even a common plant will disappear from a habitat if an essential environmental factor shifts

beyond its range of tolerance. For example, sun-loving plants, such as the common daisy, *Bellis perennis*, flourish in full sun but gradually disappear when surrounding trees and shrubs grow large enough to shade the area. In general, common plants tend to be those that have adapted to withstand a wide range of conditions, whereas rare species survive only where certain narrowly defined environmental conditions exist. It is precisely because of their narrow range of tolerance that some plants become rare. Their lack of habitat may be due to gradual changes

Above: An area of stacked logs creates a miniature ecosystem of insects and creatures that are dependent upon each other and the plants around for survival. Such creatures improve the ecological balance of wildlife gardens and kitchen gardens.

over thousands or even millions of years (such as climate change) that reduce suitable areas to a few relicts. Increasingly, however, loss of habitat is due to the actions of humans altering the environment.

Below: Every plant population attracts its own pollinators, and each exists for the mutual benefit of the other.

CONSERVING ENDANGERED SPECIES

Many plant species are now classified as endangered, because their long-term survival is under threat. There are many reasons for this, such as the erosion of a habitat, or the extinction of a key pollinator, and in some cases it is likely that the plant was never particularly numerous.

Extinction is a normal part of evolution – without it there would be no room for new species – but scientists are becoming increasingly concerned that the current rates of extinction are far above the rate at which species can easily be replaced. Attempts are therefore being made to prevent further loss of the world's rare plants.

Collecting wild plants

Though it may be tempting to pick and press wild plants, it is worth asking yourself why you want to do this. While it is true that some collections are undertaken as part of scientific research, some plants – especially the showier ones – have been overpicked to the extent that they have become critically endangered. In the UK, for instance, the lady's slipper orchid, *Cyprepedium calceolus*, was so admired by enthusiasts and collectors that it was eventually reduced to a single wild specimen. The impact of collecting one plant may seem insignificant, but the small actions of many individual collectors can lead to extinction. It is far better simply to admire the plant growing in the wild and leave it for the enjoyment of other visitors to the site.

Introduced alien plants

Many plants have become endangered because of competition from a new arrival. When plants are taken from their native environments and introduced elsewhere, they can often become highly invasive, ultimately displacing the native plants. There are numerous instances worldwide of whole native plant communities being threatened by introduced plant species.

Right: Over collection of the edelweiss, Leontopodium alpinum, *has resulted in it needing legal protection in Europe.*

Above: Collecting seeds from cultivated plants for propagation at home is accepted gardening practice, but plants growing in the wild should be left unpicked so that the population continues to thrive and support the ecosystem around it.

Climate change

It is likely that climate change will have a considerable impact on most or all ecosystems in the 21st century, and that changing weather patterns will alter the natural distribution ranges of many species or communities. If no physical barriers exist, it may be possible for species or communities to migrate. Habitats such as forest or grassland, for instance, may move to higher latitudes or higher altitudes if average temperatures increase. There is nothing new about this: at the end of the last ice age (12,000–10,000 years ago) many plant communities moved quickly north or south in response to the rapid global warming that followed.

In most cases, the real danger to habitats arises where natural or constructed barriers prevent or limit the natural movement of species or communities. Many national parks, nature reserves and protected areas are surrounded by urban or agricultural landscapes, which will prevent the migration of species beyond their current artificial boundaries.

Protected areas

Every country in the world has defined areas that are managed for the conservation of animals, plants and other natural and cultural features. Only conservation *in situ* allows the natural processes of evolution to operate on whole plant and animal communities. It permits every link in the web of life, including invertebrates, soil microbes and mycorrhiza (fungi associated with plant roots), to function and interact fully within the

Above: Bluebells have become an endangered species in the United Kingdom because of over-picking. Extinction by methods of this kind can be addressed through better public awareness.

ecosystem and is essential to allow the continued development of resistance to fungal and other diseases.

Botanic gardens and plant collections

Living collections of rare and endangered plants are a sad but necessary inclusion in many botanic gardens around the world. Their role is often indirect in relation to conservation; they serve rather to inform visitors of the danger of extinction that faces many threatened species. However, the expertise developed in growing these plants can be very useful when growing stocks for re-introduction to the wild and may improve our understanding of the needs of threatened plant species.

Seed banks ensure that plants that are currently threatened with extinction can be preserved. The seed is gathered by licensed collectors and, after careful drying and cleaning, is stored at sub-zero temperatures. The seed bank works out the best method to grow the seed so that, if the wild

plants do vanish, the species can be successfully re-introduced. Experiments and observations indicate that many seeds will survive for decades in cold storage.

Both seed banks and living collections are best viewed as a relatively short-term standby, allowing conservationists to maintain a reservoir of variation.

Re-introduction of wild plants

When plants have become rare, endangered or even extinct, it is occasionally possible to re-introduce them to areas or habitats where they formerly grew. This is rarely a simple matter, however. Its success depends on the removal of whatever pressure made the plant rare in the first place.

The café marron, *Ramosmania rodriguesii*, was thought to have been extinct for 40 years in its natural home of Rodrigues in the Indian Ocean. However, in 1980 a teacher sent his pupils out on an exploratory trip to find interesting and rare plants. One pupil unearthed a small shrub half-eaten by goats and, when he returned to the school with a cutting, the teacher identified it as the café marron. There was little hope for its future survival as it was unable to produce seeds due to a flower mutation, but recent work at the Royal Botanic Gardens at Kew in the UK has resulted in its producing seed for the first time, and it may yet be re-introduced to the wild.

Below: Botanic gardens are artificially created environments that are professionally managed for research purposes and public enjoyment. They contain native and imported species and are often nationally important.

ESTABLISHING A GRASSLAND AREA

A grassland is a windy, partly dry habitat dominated by grasses, with trees and bushes few and far between. In gardens, most grassland is shaped to form lawns, which often bear little resemblance to their wild counterpart. Wild flowers can become a feature of such an area though.

Grassland or lawn?

The commonest use of grass in the domestic garden is on a lawn. These manicured features mimic grassland in certain respects but, in many ways, the traditional lawn is quite different from its wild counterpart. In its close-cropped, well-tended state, a lawn might look good to humans but as a wildlife habitat it doesn't offer much. Changing a lawn from what is effectively a green desert to a thriving meadowland teaming with wild flowers often involves little more than reducing the amount of mowing, and outlawing the use of fertilizers, pesticides and weedkillers. This will have an almost immediate effect, but it may take some years before the full effects appear. And the time saved maintaining it can be spent more usefully elsewhere in the garden.

The importance of long grass areas

If a lawn is mown less frequently and not walked upon, other flower seeds will begin to establish. Often the species that take root first are daisies, buttercups, dandelions and small, creeping and spreading weed seeds, often the bane of the immaculate gardener's life. However leaving a strip of lawn to naturalize with other plant species can have plenty of beneficial effects for the garden, even one in which no place is usually spared for weeds to grow. Strips of uncut grass alongside a hedge, or around the base of a tree, can be planted up with wild flower species. These species encourage wildlife into the garden and they in turn will pollinate plant species. The result is a more colourful garden that containsa greater diversity of flora and a richer ecological balance.

Flower-rich grassland

Lawns that are converted into a wild flower meadow can be an important refuge for declining wild flowers, and are an excellent habitat for many insects and spiders. Lawns facing the sun are especially useful, and plants such as clover (*Trifolium*), knapweed (*Centaurea*), trefoil (*Lotus*), and vetches (*Anthyllis*, *Coronilla* and *Hippocrepis*) will encourage wildlife and they in turn will help to create a visual feast of flora.

Types of grassland

With such a wide distribution, grassland occurs in many different forms. The commonest types can be mimicked in a garden and are delightful in the late spring and early summer.

Wild flower meadow These rich flower habitats are the result of traditional management of grassland to gather hay crops. The constant removal of hay creates a poor soil.

Pasture or downland Grassland was often maintained by the constant grazing of livestock. This results in short grass that is rich in low-growing herbs.

Water meadow Sometimes called flood meadow, these are very similar to hay meadows but are flooded on a seasonal basis and so harbour different plant species.

Prairie and steppe Vast swathes of this grassland once covered large areas of the USA and Eurasia. Their rich soil supports many plant species and is a style of planting cultivated by contemporary garden designers.

Marginal grassland This simply refers to remnants of formerly extensive natural grassland and is often seen in field margins or roadsides.

Right: The combination of dazzling flowers a makes a grassland a wonderful place to visit.

Below: Spring and summer are the most spectacular time for meadows. Flowering reaches its peak at this time.

Above: Wild flowers and insects are mutually dependent, and encouraging one will automatically bring the other.

Types of wild flower lawn

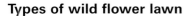

In nature, grassland is a rich and varied habitat that is moulded by the effects of geography, climate, soil and, in many cases, human intervention. Choosing the right type of grassland for your needs will depend on all these factors. Where you live will automatically decide the first three, but the last factor is mostly your choice, and depends on what you want in the garden.

Short grass or downland turf is most commonly seen in temperate regions. It is usually the result of grazing sheep, and the consequent short-cropped turf contains a multitude of flower species. It is the closest model to the modern garden lawn, and can be maintained by regular (if infrequent) cutting by a mower on a high setting.

Hay meadows are a traditional way of managing grassland for the hay that

Above: Even when you intend to let the grass grow, short-cut paths allow access to other areas of the garden and create a contrast that is visually attractive.

is cut in the summer months and stored for animal fodder. The long grass frequently harbours many species of wild flower during spring and early summer, creating an extremely pretty artificial habitat. Traditional forms of management often resulted in poor soil that reduced the vigour of the grasses and favoured the growth of wild flowers. Sadly, modern, intensive agriculture has seen a severe decline in these habitats and consequently of many wild flower species.

Wet meadows or flood meadows are largely similar to hay meadows, except that they are subject to seasonal

Below: Buttercups, once a common sight in pastureland, have become rarer with the intensification of agriculture.

flooding, usually in winter, and consequently harbour different species. All types of meadow can be established in gardens, but they need to be situated carefully and chosen appropriately and cut during the summer months, when they are not that attractive. They can be hard to establish on lawns that have been previously well fertilized.

Prairie is a term used to describe the vast areas of flower-rich grassland that once clothed North America, and is similar to the European steppe. The soils are often richer than those found in artificial meadows, and they are often full of colourful flowers, many of which have become familiar plants. The effect is potentially much easier to establish in most gardens because it depends on rich soil, with similar mowing regimes to those used in meadows.

Marginal grassland is often used to describe remnants of grassland plant communities that occur on field margins, roadsides or waste ground, and which have been marginalized. They are often a last, vital refuge for native flower species and their dependent wildlife that were formerly common in that area. The effect can be duplicated in a garden at the base of a hedge, or by leaving an occasional space. All you need do is cut it back every year or two in late winter.

CREATING A WILD FLOWER MEADOW

Wild flower meadows and flowery lawns are easy to maintain but do take some care and effort to establish. You can re-seed an area of lawn or plant pot-grown plants into existing grass. The resulting area will provide cover for insects and small animals, as well as a beautiful display of flowers.

Changing an existing lawn

The first step in transforming an existing lawn is to think about what you want the space to provide, and how much of it you want to change. If it is important to keep the same amount of grassy area, the simplest approach may be to change to wildlife-friendly maintenance. Alternatively, reduce the area of short cut lawn to a minimum, and seed or plant up the rest with wild flowers.

Assuming that you intend to keep some lawn, the simplest change is to let flowering plants colonize it. Reduce the frequency of cutting, stop fertilizing, using pesticides and weed-killers, and and stop watering it. The initial effect may be hard to see, but low-growing, broadleaved plants will soon begin to get a foothold. Even allowing areas on a clover-rich lawn to have a flowering break for a week or two will help the bees.

Making new wild flower lawns

Most grassland wild flowers grow best in poor soil with full sun and open spaces with minimal root competition from trees, so choose your site accordingly. New wild flower lawns are best grown from seed that can be bought ready mixed. Ideally, the mix will produce about 60–80 per cent grass coverage, with the remainder being wild flower. The seed mix is sown sparingly – to avoid the grasses out-competing the wild flowers – at a rate of about 15g/m^2 (½ oz per sq yd), or less.

You can also make an existing lawn richer in flowers by over-seeding in autumn with a mix of wild flower seed. To over-seed an area, cut the grass as low as possible and rake away the debris, leaving bare patches of soil among the grass. The seed is mixed with some fine, dry sand, particularly in the case of fine seed, and is thinly sown over the bare patches and then raked in lightly.

Preparing the ground and sowing wild flower meadows

1 Start by marking out the area you intend to convert to a wild flower area. Use a rope or hose to establish flowing lines and curves.

2 With the edge finalized, cut the line in the existing turf using a half-moon edging iron and following the line made by the rope.

3 Lift the existing turf, removing all grass plants, as plants growing in wild flower meadows prefer nutrient-poor soil.

4 Once the turf has been lifted, lightly cultivate the whole area with a fork, before raking it to produce a light, crumbly seed bed ready for sowing.

5 Mix the wild flowers into the grass seed prior to sowing to make it easier to distribute. Lightly sow the mix at a rate of 15g/m^2 (½ oz per sq yd).

6 The grass and wild flower seedlings will soon emerge, and the light sowing rate ensures that the grass does not swamp the developing wild flowers.

Above: Wild flower meadows offer both a habitat and a food source for bees, and are wonderfully ornamental in early summer.

The results from over-seeding can be quite variable, and many gardeners prefer to plant out pot-grown wild flowers directly into an existing lawn. Mow the lawn early in the season and scrape or use bare patches for planting into. Arrange the young plants in groups of three to nine for the best effect and maximum chances of success. Once planted, the lawn can be mown on a high setting every two to three weeks in the first year to reduce the competition from grasses. The following year, the lawn can be mown less.

Maintaining a wild flower lawn

The amount of time and effort a wild-life lawn needs will vary, depending on what you want. Shorter lawns need little change to their maintenance because the basic method of mowing remains the same, albeit less frequent.

Long grass is trickier, not least because it can be a fire hazard during dry weather. Always site an area of long grass at least 6m (20ft) away from buildings or other combustible items. A buffer zone of conventional lawn can be made more attractive by cutting the first strip of lawn next to the tall grass on the highest mower setting, and reducing this by one setting on each consecutive strip so that the longer grass blends in gradually.

Also, mowing a margin between long grass and features such as flowerbeds means that the grass will not collapse on the flowers following rain or storms. If you have a large lawn, mow a path through it so you can watch the wildlife without having to trample on the tall grass. Frequently mow areas you want to keep as paths, preventing long grass from developing and animals from sheltering there, and possibly getting killed by the blades of a lawnmower.

Hay and water meadows are usually best cut after they have stopped flowering in autumn, although if space allows you can try leaving some areas of long grass uncut until late winter to provide shelter and hibernation sites for insects and other grassland species. When you do cut the grass, remove all the clippings, usually after letting them lie for a day or two to let any wildlife caught up in them to escape, and then dispose of them elsewhere.

Top plants for a wild flower meadow

Choosing flowers for a wild flower lawn will depend on which species are native to, or will succeed best in, your area. The suggestions below give ideas for how some plants can be used; it is possible to substitute other species according to your local area.

Shorter grass

Cowslip (*Primula veris*)
An ideal plant for areas of grass that are cut somewhat infrequently, it is suited for hedge bottoms and attracts a number of insects that feed on the abundant nectar in late spring.

Harebell (*Campanula rotundifolia*)
The diminutive harebell is extremely widespread in the wild, being found across much of the northern hemisphere. It is ideal for dry sites where its flowers attract bees.

Red clover (*Trifolium pratense*)
A pea family member with round, red flowerheads that are a real favourite with bees, due to the copious nectar that they produce. Often included in agricultural mixes of grass seed because of its ability to fix nitrogen in the soil and enhance grass growth.

Long grass

Field scabious (*Knautia arvensis*)
One of the most nectar-rich of meadow flowers with pretty blue-mauve pincushions on branching stems throughout summer and well into autumn, when its seed is often eaten by birds.

Ox-eye daisy
(*Leucanthemum vulgare*)
This quick-spreading, pretty perennial produces an abundance of yellow-centred, white daisy flowers in summer. Many daisy flowers, including coneflowers (*Echinacea*), tickseed (*Coreopsis*) and asters, are suited to long grass.

Wild carrot (*Daucus carota*)
This wild ancestor of the cultivated carrot has a delicate filigree head of dainty flowers that appear in summer, and are an excellent source of food for hoverflies and butterflies.

Cowslip *Red clover* *Wild carrot* *Field scabious*

WILD FLOWER HABITATS

Flowering plants live on every continent and can be found from the ocean shores to the mountains. They are the most successful group of plants on earth, but there are very few that can boast the ability to live anywhere. Even the most widespread species have their limits and, ultimately, their preferred habitats.

Wetlands

All plants need water to live, but many species are likely to suffer and die if they get too much. If there is excessive water in the soil it forces the air out, ultimately suffocating the roots. Some plants, however, are specially adapted to living in wetlands.

Wetland plants grow in seasonally waterlogged or permanently wet conditions. There are many types of wetlands, including swamps, bogs, salt marshes, estuaries, flood plains, lakeshores and riversides. Wetlands occasionally support trees: these areas, known as wet woodland or swamp forests, are filled with rare species that tolerate wet, shady conditions.

Wetlands are rich in flowers, demonstrating that where land and

Below: A British hedgerow represents a complete ecosystem, mirroring a natural woodland edge.

water meet a rich habitat usually results. Until recently huge areas of wetland were being drained and turned into grassland or filled for development. While this continues apace in some places, wetlands are gaining a new stature in the 21st century. Many are now highly valued as natural sponges, in which water is retained on the land surface instead of flowing quickly to the sea, causing erosion and flooding as it goes.

Woodlands

Forest and woodland are extremely important habitats for many types of flowering plants, not least trees. Tree cover was once the natural vegetation over much of the Earth's surface and great forests stretched across vast tracts of every continent except Antarctica. Over the last 10,000 years

human activity has removed considerable amounts of this natural cover, particularly in Eurasia, and over the last century the trend has become a global one.

Despite the loss of forest, many areas remain and are very important havens for forest-dwelling flowers. Such flowers need to cope with low light levels for much (or even all) of the year, but trees provide a rich growing medium, through their decomposing fallen leaves, and may also provide homes for flowering climbers and epiphytes.

Exposed habitats

Where tree cover is not the dominant vegetation – whether due to human intervention or through natural

1 Chaplock	19 Hawthorn
2 Grasses	20 Long-tailed tit
3 Buttercup	21 Orange tip
4 Red clover	22 Early purple
5 Bugle	orchid
6 Chaffinch	23 Tufted vetch
7 Bramble	24 White stitchwort
8 White-tailed	25 Honeysuckle
bumblebee	26 Red campion
9 Carrion crows	27 Brimstone
10 Nettles	28 Wren
11 Dandelion	29 Field rose
12 Germander	30 Beech
13 Bluebell	31 Robin
14 Lesser celandine	32 Cow parsley
15 Garlic mustard	33 Dog violet
16 Bullfinch	34 Hoverfly
17 Kestrel	35 Primrose
18 Blackthorn	

Above: Flowers and all kinds of flora can survive in many seemingly inhospitable places.

changes – conditions are much more favourable to those species that need a lot of light. Exposed areas are mainly either grassland or scrubland and many support a truly dazzling array of wild flowers.

In temperate zones, open spaces are among the most diverse wild flower habitats to be encountered. Even open areas that are the result of human intervention, such as traditional hay meadows, are capable of supporting many flowering species. These rich habitats have become increasingly rare over the last 100 years, due mainly to agricultural improvement programmes, making those that remain precious.

Life in the extreme

In challenging locations from frozen mountain peaks to the hottest deserts, flowering plants have learned to eke out a living. Habitats of this kind are often referred to as fragile, and while the idea of a fragile desert or mountaintop may seem strange, it is entirely accurate. Extreme survival specialists are finely tuned to make the best of scarce resources. If the conditions change even slightly, plants do not always possess the right adaptations and may face extinction. Alpine plants, for instance, are much beloved by gardeners, but need specialist care, and treatment that mimics, as closely as possible, the conditions they enjoy in the wild, if they are to survive in cultivation.

SCRUBLAND AND DESERT

Much of the Earth's surface is characterized by land that is dry for much of the year. The plants that live in dry areas are specifically adapted to deal with the harsh extremes of these environments and many have become highly distinctive in appearance.

Mediterranean scrubland

Regions described as Mediterranean scrubland tend to have hot, dry summers followed by cool, moist winters. These conditions occur in the middle latitudes near continental west coasts: the Mediterranean itself, south central and south-western Australia, the fynbos of southern Africa, the Chilean matorral, and the chaparral of California. Most rainfall occurs from late autumn to early spring, and for many plants this is the prime growing and flowering season.

Although rare, this habitat features an extraordinary diversity of uniquely adapted plants – around 20 per cent of all plant species live in these regions.

Most plants that grow in these areas are fire-adapted, and actually depend on this disturbance for their survival.

Deserts

While they occur on every continent, deserts vary greatly in the amount of annual rainfall they receive and their average temperature. In general, evaporation exceeds rainfall. Many deserts, such as the Sahara, are hot all year round, but others, such as the Gobi Desert, become cold in winter.

Temperature extremes are a characteristic of most deserts. Searing daytime heat gives way to cold nights. Not surprisingly, the diversity of climatic conditions – though harsh – supports a rich array of habitats. Many are ephemeral in nature and often reflect the scarcity and

Above: Where vegetation is present, woody-stemmed shrubs, cacti and succulents tend to be characteristic of desert regions.

seasonality of available water. Despite their harsh conditions, many deserts have extraordinarily rich floras that in some cases feature high numbers of species that are endemic.

Below: Australian mallee grows at the edge of desert regions and contains plants that are both fire- and drought-resistant.

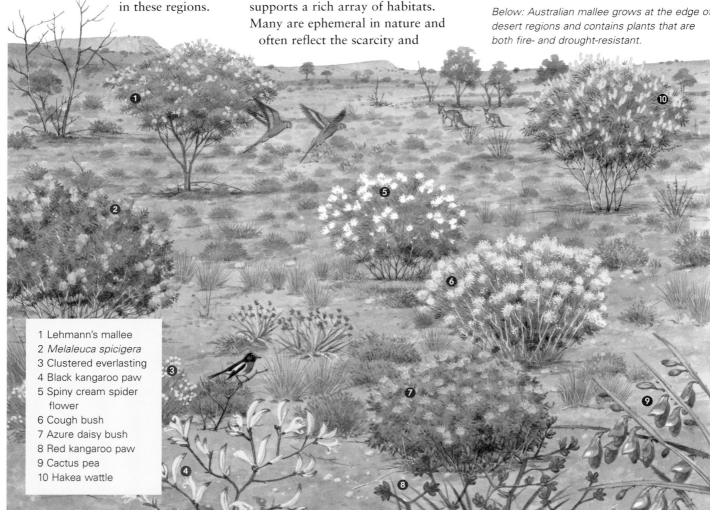

1 Lehmann's mallee
2 *Melaleuca spicigera*
3 Clustered everlasting
4 Black kangaroo paw
5 Spiny cream spider flower
6 Cough bush
7 Azure daisy bush
8 Red kangaroo paw
9 Cactus pea
10 Hakea wattle

CONIFEROUS WOODLAND

Among the most ancient of flowering plants, conifers once dominated the whole of the Earth's surface. In modern times, however, they have become more restricted as broad-leaved flowering plants have become the dominant group.

Boreal forest

Also known as taiga or northern coniferous forest, boreal forest is located south of tundra and north of temperate deciduous forests or grass-lands. Vast tracts of this forest span northern North America, Europe and Asia. Boreal forests cover around 17 per cent of the Earth's surface. They are characterized by a cold, harsh climate, low rainfall or snowfall and a short growing season. They may be open woodlands with widely spaced trees or dense forests whose floor is in shade. The dominant ground cover is mosses and lichens, with a few specialized flowering plants.

Above: Coniferous woodland has a simple structure, a canopy layer and an understorey.

Tropical coniferous forest

Found predominantly in North and Central America, in tropical regions that experience low levels of rain and moderate variability in temperature, these forests feature a thick, closed canopy, which blocks light to the floor and allows little to grow beneath. The ground is covered with fungi and ferns and is usually relatively poor in flowering plants.

Temperate rainforest

In temperate regions, evergreen forests are found in areas with warm summers and cool winters. Conifers dominate some, while others are characterized by broadleaved evergreen trees.

Temperate evergreen forests are common in the coastal areas of regions that have mild winters and heavy rainfall, or in mountain areas. Temperate conifer forests sustain the highest levels of plant material in any land habitat and are notable for trees that often reach massive proportions.

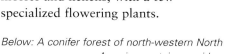

Below: A conifer forest of north-western North America contains a wide variety of flowering plants.

1 Dogwood
2 Fireweed
3 Meadow goldenrod
4 Tiger lily
5 Calypso
6 Bunchberry
7 Yellow fawn lilies
8 Wood nymph
9 Rocky mountain lilies
10 Spring beauty
11 Dwarf waterleaf

HEDGEROWS

Many agricultural landscapes are defined by hedgerows, which are important habitats for many plants. A hedgerow is formed of a row of intermeshing shrubs and bushes and sometimes trees that form a boundary to keep in livestock, and are home to a diverse range of creatures.

Though a product of human activity, not all hedgerows were planted: they are sometimes relics of former habitats and may even be the oldest feature in a landscape, providing important evidence of its historic development. In the UK, for instance, the oldest hedges are probably the remains of the ancient woodland that used to cover most of the country. As villagers and landowners cleared the forest for agricultural purposes, they would leave the last narrow strip of woodland to mark the outer boundaries of their land.

Species diversity

At the heart of an ancient hedgerow is a dense shrub layer; at intervals along it trees form a broken canopy. At ground level a rich layer of herbs grows along the base of the hedge, at

Above: Hedgrows are the corridors in which small animals, such as mice, thrive, and are home to a myriad of insects and birds.

the field edge. The older the hedgerow, the greater diversity of animal and plant life it will support. The easiest way to age a hedge is to mark out a 30m/33yd stretch, then count the number of different species of trees and shrubs it contains. It is reckoned to take about a hundred years for each woody plant to establish itself, so for each different species you find you can add a century to the age of the hedge.

Hedgerows are very important habitats as they combine the characteristics of two other habitats – woodlands and

Below: Hedgerows combine attributes of merging habitats.

1 Dog rose
2 Honeysuckle
3 Lesser celandine
4 Red campion
5 Foxglove
6 Blackthorn

open fields. They are "corridors" for wildlife, allowing species to disperse and move from one habitat area to another. While it is difficult for most plants to spread across open fields, they can "travel" along the base of a hedge, which is often their only realistic refuge.

Below: Hedgerows are safe places in which birds can nest. The presence of eggs suggests a healthy hedgerow.

Vanishing hedgerows

The agricultural policies of recent decades have led to concern about the rate at which hedgerows are disappearing. Between 1984 and 1993, the length of managed hedgerows in the UK alone decreased by nearly a third. Hedgerow loss occurs not only when hedges are deliberately removed to make larger fields, but also when they are left to become derelict: if they are not regularly cut and managed, they grow into open lines of bushes and trees.

Pesticide or fertilizer damage can be a particular problem on intensively managed farmland, where weedkillers have often been applied to hedge bottoms to eliminate weeds. This has proved to be a very damaging practice for the natural wild flower population of hedgerows. Almost as damaging is fertilizer "drift" (unintentional overspill) into the hedge base, as it promotes the growth of certain plant species at the expense of others. Often, the species that are favoured are of little conservation value. As well as losing valuable flowers the animals that live in this environment perish.

Above: Hedgerows are often rich in species that have been driven from much of the surrounding landscape.

Above: Mice thrive in hedgerows that are maintained organically. They are part of the chain of life that helps to disperse seeds to another area of land.

BROAD-LEAVED FOREST

Many types of forest can be classified as broad-leaved. The principal types are temperate lowland forests, tropical rainforests and cloud forests, and tropical and sub-tropical dry forests. All of these typically have large, broad-leaved trees as their dominant vegetation.

There is considerable variation between forests of different types and in different locations in respect of the wild flowers they contain.

Temperate deciduous forest

The forests that tend to grow in cool, rainy areas are characterized by trees that lose their leaves in the autumn. By shedding its leaves, a tree conserves resources and avoids the hardship of maintaining its foliage through the cold, dark winter. Before falling, the leaves often turn brilliant colours, ranging from red to orange to yellow to brown, as the tree withdraws the chlorophyll and other useful substances from them. Once on the forest floor they decompose and enrich the soil.

Many low-growing plants that live in these areas commonly take advantage of the winter and early spring periods when the trees are bare. During this time the absence of shade allows them to complete their life cycle in a few months while (for them at least) light levels are highest. In late spring, when the trees have regrown their leaves, the forest floor is once again in deep shade. The seed of some species waits in the soil until trees fall, or are felled, before it germinates and grows in the resulting clearing. These plants may make a dense, showy stand for a few years before the forest

canopy, often far above the ground, closes once more and shades them out.

Temperate deciduous forests are found around the globe in the middle latitudes: in the Northern Hemisphere they grow in North America, Europe and eastern Asia, and in the Southern Hemisphere there are smaller areas, in South America, southern Africa, Australia and New Zealand. They have four distinct seasons – spring, summer, autumn and winter – and the growing season for trees in temperate forests lasts about six months.

Tropical rainforest

Very dense, warm and wet, rainforests are located in the tropics – a wide band around the equator, mostly in the area between the Tropic of Cancer (23.5° N) and the Tropic of Capricorn (23.5° S). They grow in South America, West Africa, Australia, southern India and South-east Asia.

A fairly warm, consistent temperature, coupled with a high level of rainfall, characterizes tropical rainforests. They are dominated by semi-evergreen and evergreen tree species. These number in the thousands and contribute to the highest levels of species diversity of any major terrestrial habitat type. Overall, rainforests are home to more species than any other forest habitat.

Dry forest

Tropical and sub-tropical dry forests are found in Central and South America, Africa and Madagascar, India, Indochina, New Caledonia and the Caribbean. Though they occur in climates that are warm all year round and may receive heavy rain for part of the year, they also have long dry seasons that last several months. Deciduous trees are the dominant vegetation in these forests.

Below and right: In the Northern Hemisphere, bluebells take advantage of the extra light in spring, when trees are bare, in order to grow and flower. They finish flowering just as the tree canopy above starts to fill in.

1 ❶

1 Bluebells

GRASSLAND

Windy and partly dry, grassland generally lacks woody vegetation, and the dominant plant type is, of course, grasses. Almost one quarter of the Earth's land surface is grassland, and in many areas grassland is the major habitat separating forests from deserts.

Grasslands, also known as savanna, pampas, campo, plain, steppe, prairie and veldt, can be divided into two types – temperate and tropical.

Temperate grassland

Located north of the Tropic of Cancer and south of the Tropic of Capricorn, temperate grasslands are common throughout these ranges. They experience a range of seasonal climatic variations typified by hot summers and cold winters. The combination of open, windy sites and dense stands of grasses mean that the evaporation rate is high, so little of the rain that falls reaches the rich soil.

The extraordinary floral communities of the Eurasian steppes and the North American plains have been largely destroyed due to the conversion of these lands to agriculture. In surviving areas of North American tall-grass prairie, as many as 300 different plant species may grow in 1 hectare/2.5 acres.

Tropical grassland

The annual temperature regime in tropical grassland is quite different to that of temperate grassland: in tropical regions it is hot all year, with wet seasons that bring torrential rains interspersed with drier seasons. Tropical grasslands are located between the Tropic of Cancer and the Tropic of Capricorn and are sometimes collectively called savannas. Many savannas do have scattered trees, and often occur between grassland and forest. They are predominantly located in the dry tropics and the subtropics, often bordering a rainforest. The plant diversity of these regions is typically lower than that of other tropical habitats and of temperate grassland.

Montane grassland

At high elevations around the world montane grasslands occur. They are found in tropical, subtropical and temperate regions, and the plants they contain often display striking adaptations to cool, wet conditions and intense sunlight, including features such as rosette structures or waxy surfaces on their leaves or stems. In the tropics these habitats are highly distinctive: examples include the heathlands and moorlands of Mount Kilimanjaro and Mount Kenya in East Africa, Mount Kinabalu in Borneo, and the Central Range of New Guinea, all of which support ranges of endemic plants.

Flooded grassland

Common to four of the continents, flooded grassland (as the name suggests) is a large expanse or complex of grassland flooded by either rain or river, usually as part of a seasonal cycle. These areas support numerous plants adapted to wet conditions. The Florida Everglades, for example, which contain the world's largest rain-fed flooded grassland, are home to some 11,000 species of flowering plants.

Below: Characteristic plants of montane grasslands display features such as rosette structures, waxy leaf or stem surfaces.

1 Iris
2 Feverfew
3 Anemone
4 Yellow asphodel

FIELDS

Farmland, fields or paddocks are essentially an environment constructed by humans, who have altered the natural landscape for the purposes of agriculture. The general term "pasture" describes grassland, rough grazing land and traditionally managed hay meadows.

Rough pasture

There are two types of pasture – permanent and rough. Permanent pasture is closed in, fertilized and sown with commercial grass species. It is often treated with herbicides that allow only a few species of grass to grow, so that it does not support a wide range of wildlife species. Rough pasture is usually much older and is typically land that is very difficult to plough so is left undisturbed.

Pasturelands owe their existence to farm livestock, and are very sensitive habitats that can easily be over- or undergrazed. They generally contain a single early stage of native vegetation, which is prevented from developing further by grazing; if the animals are removed, shrubs quickly establish and woodland develops soon afterwards. This is because many livestock animals graze very close to the ground and, while this does not damage grasses (which regrow from just above their roots), many taller plants cannot tolerate it. Grazing animals also

Above: California poppies and lupines form colourful swathes in North American grasslands.

remove nutrients from the environment so many traditional grassland areas are fairly infertile.

The wildflowers of pasture are species that grow low and thus avoid being eaten by animals. They may creep or form low rosettes of leaves and, although diminutive in general, they often have large, showy flowers that readily attract pollinators.

Below: Pasture that has been left undisturbed and unmanaged is full of life, some of which may be readily found only in that habitat.

Meadows

A true meadow is a field in which the grasses and other plants are allowed to grow in the summer and are then cut to make hay. The plants are cut while still green and then left in the field to dry. In many countries this has been the traditional method of providing feed for cattle during the winter. Hay meadows support a huge range of wild flowers, some of which have become extremely rare as traditional haymaking has been superseded by modern farming methods.

Crop fields

Many fields are used to grow crops other than grass, such as grains or vegetables. In these situations, weed species often find the conditions to their liking and thrive there. Many of these are annual flowers and some – such as cornflowers, *Centaurea cyanus*, or poppies, *Papaver rhoeas*, in wheat fields – are colourful additions to the agricultural landscape.

1 Poppy
2 Oxeye daisy
3 Hedge wound wort
4 Buttercup

HEATHS

Heaths are open landscapes that are usually treeless. Their vegetation consists largely of dwarf woody shrubs such as heathers. They are divided into two main types: upland heath (usually called moorland) and lowland heath.

Lowland heath

These habitats are under threat. They are restricted to the British Isles, northern Germany, southern Scandinavia and adjacent, mainly coastal, parts of western Europe, but equivalent vegetation types occur in cooler regions elsewhere in the world.

Lowland heath usually occurs where forest cover has been removed, usually as a result of human action, so to a large extent this is a habitat created by people. However, it can also occur on the drying surfaces of blanket bogs and fenland. In all cases, the soil under heathland is poor, with most of the nutrients having been leached from the topsoil by water. Heathland also occurs near the sea. Coastal heaths are more likely to be the result of natural factors such as the soil type and especially the exposure to high wind, which suppresses tree growth.

Above: Coastal heathlands are often exposed to high winds that cause a stunted growth.

Climate and soil

For lowland heath to occur, the climate must be "oceanic", with relatively high annual rainfall (60–110cm/24–43in) spread evenly throughout the year. The relative humidity remains moderately high even in the driest months. Winters are rarely very cold and summers rarely get very hot.

The continuous rain seeping into and through the soil promotes leaching (the loss of plant nutrients) and soils are poor as a result. If forest establishes in these areas it does not suffer

from this nutrient loss – trees can maintain virtually all their nutrients within the living vegetation. It is possible that slow nutrient loss from a forest ecosystem will eventually lead to a patchwork of forest, scrub and heath. Under normal circumstances, either grazing or fires are necessary to prevent the re-invasion by scrub or colonizer tree species.

Plant adaptations

The term "heath" is derived from the heather plant, and heathers, *Erica* species, form a major part of the vegetation. Heathlands are mostly species-poor. All the species that are present in a given area ultimately look remarkably similar. In open and often windswept conditions all the species present will possess minute leaves with adaptations such as sunken stomata to minimize water loss through transpiration.

Below: Heathland is often species-rich despite the poor soils.

1 Oak
2 Euphorbia
3 Lavender
4 Juniper
5 Broom
6 Strawberry tree
7 Thyme
8 Rosemary

MOUNTAINS AND MOORLAND

Collectively, mountains and upland areas make up around 20 per cent of the world's landscape, and about 80 per cent of our fresh water originates in them. Upland heath, or moorland, occurs at altitudes above 300m/1,000ft in most temperate zones but may be found at much higher altitudes in the tropics.

Mountains

All mountain ranges feature rapid changes in altitude, climate, soil, and vegetation over very short distances. The temperature can change from extremely hot to below freezing in a matter of a few hours. Mountain habitats harbour some of the world's most unusual plants, and collectively they are home to a huge range of species. This diversity is due to their range of altitude, which results in distinct belts, or zones, of differing climates, soils and plantlife.

Vegetation on a mountain typically forms belts. This is because as the altitude increases the temperature steadily decreases – by about 2°C per 300m/3.5°F per 1,000ft. This, coupled with the thinning of the atmosphere, leads to unusually high levels of

Left: Mountain vegetation often forms distinct belts according to the altitude.

ultraviolet light and means that as plants grow higher on the mountainside they need special adaptations to survive. Typically as the altitude increases the plant species become increasingly distinct.

Below: Mountains are often isolated habitats and may contain a unique diversity of species.

Moorland and upland heath

The vegetation in moorland regions is similar in character to that of lowland heath, but it grows on deep layers of peaty or other organic soil. Moorland characteristically occurs below the alpine belt and (usually) above the tree line. It is typically dominated by dwarf shrubs, such as heather, over an understorey of small herbs and mosses.

Natural moorlands (those which are largely unmanaged by people) are generally diverse habitats, containing stands of vegetation at different stages of growth. Animal grazing and burning may be the only factors preventing them from developing into scrub or woodland.

1 Gladiolus
2 Lobelia wollastonii
3 Protea
4 Giant groundsel
5 Saxifrage
6 Umbellifer
7 Mosses

TUNDRA AND ALPINE HABITATS

In the areas nearest the poles, and in the high mountainous places of the world, the conditions for plant growth become extreme. These cold, often frozen, environments present plants with a real challenge that only the hardiest species can withstand.

Cold places

The predominant habitat in the outer polar regions and on mountaintops is known as tundra. Although arctic and alpine (mountain) tundra display differences, they often support plants with similar adaptations.

Tundra is a cold, treeless area, with very low temperatures, little rain or snow, a short growing season, few nutrients and low species diversity. It is the coldest habitat to support plant life.

Arctic tundra

The frozen, windy, desert-like plains of the arctic tundra are found in the far north of Greenland, Alaska, Canada, Europe and Russia, and also in some sub-Antarctic islands. The long, dry winters of the polar regions feature months of total darkness and extreme cold, with temperatures dipping as low as -51°C/-60°F. The average annual temperature is -12– -6°C/ 10–20°F. The annual precipitation is very low, usually amounting to less than 25cm/10in. Most of this falls as snow during the winter and melts at the start of the brief summer growing season. However, a layer of permafrost (frozen subsoil), usually within 1m/3ft of the surface, means that there is very little drainage, so bogs and ponds dot the surface and provide moisture for plants. The short growing season, when the sun gains enough strength to melt the ice, lasts for only 50–60 days. Ironically, the surface snow that marks the end of the growing season acts as an insulating blanket, ensuring that the plants do not freeze solid in winter.

The tundra supports communities of sedges and heaths as well as dwarf shrubs. Most of these plants are slow-growing and have a creeping habit, interweaving to form a low springy mass. This adaptation helps to avoid the icy winds and lessen the chances of being eaten by large grazing animals.

Above: Despite their harshness, tundra and alpine regions often support showy species.

Alpine tundra

Above the tree line and below the permanent snow line, alpine tundra is located high in mountains worldwide. In contrast to the arctic tundra, the soil of alpine tundra is very well drained and may become quite dry during the growing season, which lasts for about 180 days. Nighttime temperatures are usually below freezing.

Below: The tundra's short growing season often results in brief but dazzling displays of colour.

1 Cotton grass
2 Arctic poppy
3 Arctic forget-me-not
4 Cinquefoil

CLIFFS AND ROCKY SHORES

Rocky coasts and cliffs occur where the underlying rocks are relatively resistant to the constant pounding of the sea, rain and wind. They are found along coasts. Often the landscape is one of grandeur, characterized by steep cliffs, rocky outcrops and small bays with deep, usually clear, offshore waters.

Coastlines

Rocky coasts are often quite exposed and the constant exposure to salt-laden winds, coupled with a shortage of soil in which plant roots can anchor themselves, reduces the range of plants to a few specialist species.

Cliffs

Coastal cliffs, especially those in exposed locations, are often drenched in salt spray as the sea is driven on to the shore. Plants that grow above the spray line, out of reach of the waves and regular salt spray, are likely to be salt-tolerant, whereas those on the beach at the bottom of a cliff, or in rock crevices that are sometimes washed by salt spray, must be tolerant of salt to survive. Plants rarely grow near the base of cliffs that rise directly from the sea because the high wave energy prevents them from becoming established.

Above: Many coastal plants, such as thrift, flower profusely despite their small size.

The exposure and lack of soil in all but the deeper rock crevices means that the plants that live on cliffs often face a similar challenge to those found in the higher rocky areas in mountain ranges. This is why they often show similar adaptations, such as deep roots, creeping or hummocky growth habit and the ability to withstand exposure and drought.

The rocky coast may include indentations known as fjords, formed by glaciers wearing away depressions that were subsequently flooded by the rising water following the end of the last ice age, 10,000 years ago. These fjords may have salt marshes at their head and may be surrounded by steep-sided wooded slopes, creating a rich and varied habitat.

Rocky shores

Bedrock outcrops and boulders dominate rocky shores. The lower zones of the rocks are flooded and exposed daily by the tides and support only marine plants, whereas the upper zones are flooded during unusually high tides or in strong storms. In spite of being frequently washed by seawater, salt-tolerant land plants survive here by being well rooted in crevices in the lower-lying rocks.

Below: The high winds of coastal regions mean that plants growing there are often short and ground hugging.

1 Sea lavender
2 Thrift
3 Cornish heath
4 Sea aster

BEACHES AND SAND DUNES

Coastlines are often areas of extreme biological diversity. Areas where one habitat meets another always offer an array of flora and fauna, as animals and plants from both habitats merge. Beaches may seem like the exception where plants are concerned, as they often have limited vegetation.

Beaches

Generally, beaches are made up of sand, gravel, cobbles (shingle) and fragments of seashells, corals or other sea creatures. The proportions of all of these vary from beach to beach. Level areas of sand that are exposed only during low tide are called sandflats. Although an amazing variety of animals thrive in this habitat, very few flowering plants survive, mainly because of wave action and the saltiness of seawater. Those that do grow on them usually occur near the high tide line.

Sand dunes

Usually occuring immediately inland from sandy beaches, sand dunes are found in many parts of the world but are less well developed in tropical and subtropical coastal zones, due to lower wind speeds and damper sand. There

Above: The salty conditions and unstable sandy soil can be challenging for plants.

Above: The showy flowerheads of sea holly, Eryngium maritimum, *are common on dunes.*

are exceptions, however, such as the vast desert dune expanses of the Namib Desert in south-western Africa.

Sand is blown from the beach and initially accumulates in a characteristic steep windward face and more gently sloping leeward face. A change to dune meadow or dune heath eventually happens as grasses establish and stabilize the dune system, usually some

way inland. These dune slacks become dominated by low scrub, which rarely exceeds 90cm/3ft in height and is often much smaller. A few larger shrubby species are also capable of invading sand dunes to form scrub and can ultimately revert to woodland.

Below: Sand dunes are mobile, and may shift by several metres per year.

1 Sea rocket
2 Sea holly
3 Sea spurge
4 Sea bindweed
5 Yellow horned poppy
6 Burnet rose

RIVERSIDES AND WETLANDS

Wetlands are being lost at an alarming rate and many species that live in them are suffering. The habitats along rivers, waterholes and streams are critical landscapes: they help to maintain water quality and the shape and form of streams, as well as supporting species diversity in surrounding habitats.

Riversides

In their upper reaches, rivers are fast flowing with no vegetation in the water, although bankside vegetation is usually present. In the lower reaches, the water is calmer, and floating leaved and semi-aquatic plants can survive.

Riverside habitats are diverse. Grazed riverside pastures, flood meadows, marshes, reedbeds and riverine forest are common features beside many rivers, although the natural richness of the soil in the river flood plain has led people to cultivate and plant crops right to the edge of the

Below: Rivers are often home to a rich and varied selection of plant and animal life.

water in many regions. Rivers may also be altered, with their curves straightened and banks raised to create flood defences. All these factors mean that truly natural riverside habitats are scarce in areas of human occupation.

Wetlands

Marshes and flood meadows are low-lying wet areas that often flood on a seasonal basis. Reedbeds occur on land that is flooded for most of the year, often at the edges of lakes or in shallow lagoons, and often support a very diverse range of plants. Fens are areas where peat has been deposited over a long period and are often associated with extensive tracts of

Above: Reedbeds are often home to a rich diversity of plant and animal species.

marshes and reedbeds. They may contain large areas of open water and shallow, slow-flowing rivers, and are found on ground that is permanently, seasonally or periodically waterlogged.

1 Coral plant
2 Bromeliads
3 Vriesia
4 Flowering tree
5 Vridia
6 Bromeliad
7 Passion flower
8 Heliconia
9 Orchid
10 Strelitzia
11 Orchid
12 Rosy orchid

ESTUARIES, SWAMPS AND COASTAL MARSHES

Rivers eventually end by flowing out into the sea. As the river slows, the material that it has carried in the water is deposited, and sedimentary deltas, wetlands, lagoons, salt marshes and swamps may be formed.

River mouth habitats are usually extremely diverse and include abundant and rare species.

Deltas
A delta is formed where a river flows into a calm sea. As the river slows down it drops its sediment, which builds up over years to create a delta. Over time, the river splits into smaller channels called distributaries. Occasionally this can happen inland where a river flows into a low-lying basin. It forms an immense low-lying wetland, such as that of the Okavango Delta in Botswana, Africa.

Below: Tropical and subtropical marshlands are home to many beautiful plant species.

Above: Saltwater marshes are among the most productive habitats on earth.

Marshes and swamps
Salt marshes are made up of plant communities that are tolerant of being submerged for short periods by the tide. They can be "transitional zones", which merge with nearby areas of reed swamp, sand dune, shingle, freshwater wetland or woodland, and are particularly rich in a wide variety of plants. They are often brackish (less salty than the sea but saltier than the river) and may contain a mixture of riverside and coastal vegetation types.

The term "swamp" is usually applied to warm, wet areas that are teeming with both animal and plant life. They are often (but by no means always) heavily forested, with trees that are highly adapted to waterlogged ground. Some of these areas may be very extensive and include both coastal and freshwater habitat, such as are found in the Florida Everglades.

Mangroves are marine tidal forests that are generally most luxuriant around the mouths of large rivers or sheltered bays, growing in both salt and freshwater. They are found mainly in the tropics where annual rainfall is fairly high.

1 Bald cypress
2 Floating hearts
3 Scarlet ladies tresses
4 *Thalia dealbata*
5 Sawgrass
6 Palmetto
7 Water spider orchid
8 Ghost flower orchid
9 Night fragrance orchid
10 Golden club
11 Water lettuce

OPEN WATER

Flowering plants face possibly their biggest challenge in open water. Plants living in this environment must be able to survive either submerged beneath or floating on the surface of a body of water, and all are specially adapted to allow them to do this.

Obtaining sufficient oxygen is the greatest problem facing plants that live in water. The muddy sediment at the water bottom has few air spaces, and therefore barely any oxygen present.

Lakes and ponds

A lake describes any large body of fresh water, ranging from small ponds to huge bodies of water. They can be an extremely variable habitat, ranging from almost lifeless, acidic mountain tarns to lowland lakes teeming with life. Lakes are closely associated with rivers, chiefly because some lakes are the source for rivers. Both are fresh

Below: Although certain plant species have evolved to live in the water, the richest diversity occurs where land and water meet.

Above: Open water is a challenging habitat for plants to survive in.

water and share similar characteristics, and many species are common to both habitats.

A pond is a body of water shallow enough to support rooted plants, which in time may grow all the way across it.

Slow-flowing rivers and streams

When rivers flow slowly they may support aquatic plants in a similar way to lakes. Plants that grow in slow-flowing rivers will be species that are able to root into the bottom sediment, to stop them being washed away.

As the river runs more slowly it warms up, favouring plant growth, though in areas where the banks are tree-lined this can reduce plant growth in the water. Some river plants are only semi-aquatic, growing out of the water on the bank when the stream dries up, before being re-flooded during rainy seasons.

1 Great willow herb
2 Flowering rush
3 Branched bur weed
4 Water crowfoot
5 White water lilies
6 Reed sweet grass
7 Yellow flag iris
8 Marsh marigold
9 Hemlock water dropwort
10 Marsh thistle
11 Bullrush

THE WORLD OF WILD FLOWERS

Australia is an ancient continent, with a continuous history

of 200 million years above sea level, and is home to a great many

species of flowering plants, more than two-thirds of which are not

found anywhere else on Earth. The Pacific Ocean covers nearly one-third

of the globe, and is the largest, deepest and probably the most violent of

all oceans. Its vast central and southern expanse – known as Oceania –

is dotted with many thousands of islands. Many of these islands are

home to unusual and interesting plants, all of which originally reached

them from across the ocean, although many have since evolved into

unique forms. The region does not include any continental land mass,

although Australia and New Zealand are sometimes included on

its westernmost edge.

Above from left: Willow-leaved crowea (Crowea saligna)*, ivory curl* (Buckinghamia celsissima)*, and lesser bottlebrush* (Callistemon phoeniceus)*.*

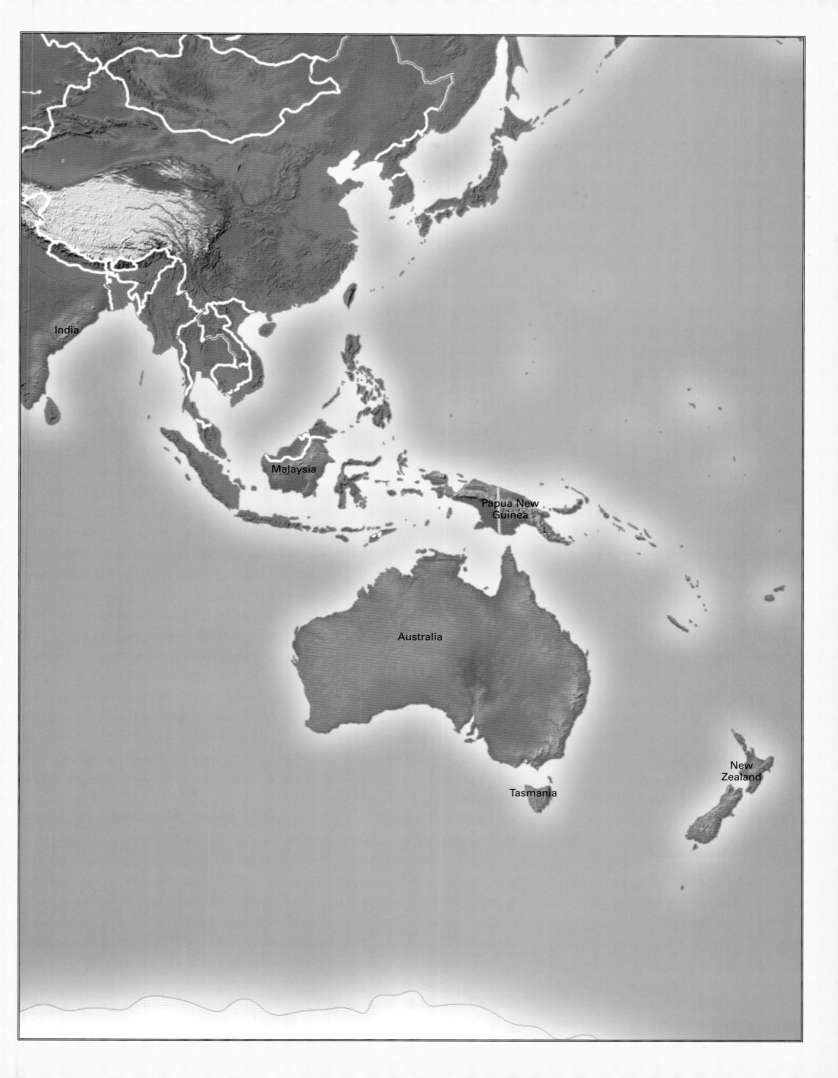

BUTTERCUP AND DILLENIA FAMILIES

The Ranunculaceae, or buttercup family, is better represented in the Northern Hemisphere than in Australasia or Oceania, but those that do occur are often striking examples within the family. The Dilleniaceae, or dillenia family, is closely related, mainly from tropical and warm regions, especially Australia. It includes trees, shrubs and occasionally vines, comprising 10 genera and about 350 species.

Gold Guinea Plant

Snake vine, climbing guinea flower, *Hibbertia scandens*

This climbing shrub is restricted to eastern Australia, occurring in Queensland and New South Wales. It climbs by twining its way up other shrubs and may occur as a more procumbent shrub in the absence of a suitable support plant. Its large golden-yellow flowers are borne at the end of short side branches and appear in early spring among the evergreen leaves, often providing an eye-catching display among the shrubby vegetation.

Below: Berries cluster on old sepals.

Identification: The trailing stems of this vigorous climber are initially hairy. The leaves are alternate, 5–10cm/2–4in long, glossy above and hairy beneath, and tend to clasp the stems. The golden-yellow flowers, which have an unpleasant smell, are up to 5cm/2in across and are borne at the tips of downy, lateral branchlets; they have five notched petals with slightly wavy edges, and numerous stamens. The round fruits, about 2cm/¾in across, contain several shiny red seeds.

Distribution: Eastern Australia.
Height and spread: 1.8m/6ft.
Habit and form: Evergreen shrub.
Leaf shape: Obovate to lanceolate.
Pollinated: Insect.

Far left: The short side branches are laden with flowers in early spring.

Korikori

Hairy alpine buttercup, *Ranunculus insignis*

This yellow-flowered New Zealand buttercup is found at higher altitudes of around 1,050–2,000m/3,500–6,500ft on North and South Islands. It is a widespread species but generally tends to favour habitats that are sheltered from the drying sun: in areas with a greater number of cloudy days it can be found in more exposed positions, but always prefers moist soils.

Right: The large leathery leaves can easily be spotted in high rocky places when the plant is not in flower.

Identification: The stems range in height from 10–90cm/4–36in. The dark green, leathery, basal leaves, up to 15cm/6in across, are oval to heart-shaped, with toothed, hairy margins; the stem leaves have three lobes. Each branched stem carries numerous yellow flowers up to 5cm/2in across, with five to seven oval, notched or rounded petals.

Below right: The yellow flowers are borne abundantly above the large leaves (below).

Distribution: New Zealand.
Height and spread: 10–90cm/4–36in.
Habit and form: Herbaceous perennial.
Leaf shape: Ovate-cordate.
Pollinated: Insect.

Mount Cook Lily

Mountain buttercup, *Ranunculus lyallii*

This magnificent buttercup, from the Southern Alps of New Zealand's South Island, has large, waxy white flowers held above huge glossy leaves shaped like saucers. It prefers a sheltered site, usually in the shade of rocks or other plants, and flourishes in stony soils near torrents at altitudes of 450–1,500m/1,500–5,000ft. It is an extremely robust plant in ideal conditions and can be very striking when encountered in the wild.

Distribution: South Island, New Zealand.
Height and spread: Up to 1.5m/5ft.
Habit and form: Herbaceous perennial.
Leaf shape: Peltate.
Pollinated: Insect.

Far right: The large distinctive, saucer-shaped leaves stand out among rocks and other mountain plants.

Identification: The stout, branched stems may grow up to 1.5m/5ft tall. The saucer-shaped leaves are dark green and leathery, borne on long stalks attached to the centre of the leaves; the basal leaves are up to 40cm/16in across, progressively reducing in size up the stems. The white flowers are borne in panicles of 5–15; they are 5–7.5cm/2–3in across with 10–16 oval, rounded or notched petals and a green centre surrounded by numerous yellow stamens.

OTHER BUTTERCUP AND DILLENIA SPECIES OF NOTE

Twining Guinea Flower
Hibbertia dentata
This trailing or twining shrub found in New South Wales, has large, deep yellow flowers with oval pointed petals, alternating with shortened calyx lobes, which appear on the branch ends. The dark green leaves are prickle-toothed.

Trailing Guinea Flower *Hibbertia empetrifolia*
This small shrub occurs naturally in a wide variety of habitats in south-east Australia, from south-east Queensland around the coast to South Australia and Tasmania. The yellow flowers appear in spring, and at their peak the plants resemble bright yellow mounds, with the foliage scarcely visible between the flowers.

Ranunculus pinguis
This New Zealand native, found only on the Auckland Islands and Campbell Island is now restricted to a few, rather inaccessible ledges, due to intensive grazing. The multi-petalled yellow flowers appear in the spring above the basal leaves, which resemble pelargonium leaves.

Old Man's Beard *Clematis aristata*
This Australian climber flowers in early summer in panicle-like inflorescences arising from leaf axils near the branch tips. The showy flowers consist of four or five white or ivory sepals. These are followed later in the season by feathery, fluffy seedheads.

Small-leaved Clematis

Traveller's joy, *Clematis microphylla*

This vigorous, sprawling climber is widespread in Australia, and is found in all states except the Northern Territory. It is especially common in coastal regions or near rivers, in moist gullies and on tablelands. The species is dioecious, with male and female flowers carried on separate plants. The greenish-white flowers, which appear in early summer, are produced in the leaf axils, giving the branch tips an inflorescence-like appearance when the plant is in full bloom.

Distribution: Australia.
Height and spread: 3m/10ft.
Habit and form: Woody, sprawling climber.
Leaf shape: Trifoliate, lanceolate.
Pollinated: Insect.

Identification: The leaves are opposite, on long leaf stalks, often twisted; each consists of two or three narrow or lance-shaped leaflets about 15mm/⅝in long and 3mm/⅛in wide. The star-like flowers, carried in short panicles, consist of four narrow, creamy-white sepals tinged green, up to 2.5cm/1in long, surrounding a central mass of numerous yellow stamens. They are followed by attractive, feathery seedheads on the female plants.

Above and below: The seedheads appear in late summer and autumn.

ROSE, PITTOSPORUM AND TREMANDRA FAMILIES

The rose family, Rosaceae, has a worldwide distribution. In contrast, the Pittosporaceae, or pittosporum family, with nine genera and 240 species from the tropical world, is centred on Australasia, and the Tremandaceae (tremenda family), with three genera and 43 species, are found in temperate Australia.

Creeping Lawyer

Snow raspberry, *Rubus parvus*

This scrambling, thorny, shrubby perennial is restricted to the north-west of New Zealand's South Island. It is most commonly found in lowland forest and river flats, where its thorny stems and bronzed foliage form tangled masses over the ground. The white flowers appear in the summer and are followed by juicy, edible, red "blackberry" fruits. It is one of only a few evergreen shrubs in New Zealand that develop an autumn tint to the foliage. Hikers know it as a plant that is "easy to get involved with, but difficult to shake off".

Identification: The smooth stems, rooting at the nodes, are usually without prickles when mature. The leathery leaves are narrow to lance-shaped, up to 16mm/⅝in long, dark green turning bronze in the autumn, shiny above, dull below, densely and regularly serrated, with small sharp teeth on the underside of the midrib; they are borne on prickly leaf stalks up to 2.5cm/1in long. White flowers, up to 2.5cm/1in across, appear in summer in small panicles; they have five oval, spreading petals and numerous stamens. The red fruits are up to 2.5cm/1in long.

Distribution: South Island, New Zealand.
Height and spread: Variable.
Habit and form: Prostrate, scrambling, evergreen shrub.
Leaf shape: Lanceolate.
Pollinated: Insect.

Left: The thorny stems form a tangled mass that spreads over the ground.

Above left: The fruits are edible.

White Marianthus

Marianthus candidus

This twining shrub is endemic to western Australia, on limestone plains, particularly in coastal heaths, south from Perth to Cape Leeuwin. The dense white flower clusters appear mainly in the spring and are very attractive. The sharply pointed white petals become pink with age, especially on the lower side, and the narrow, erect, claw-like anthers are covered in bright blue pollen.

Below White marianthus thrives in sandy soil.

Right: This plant is a twining shrub or vine that grows to 5m/16ft.

Identification: The erect, eventually twining stems are warty with lenticels. The mature leaves are narrow, up to 7cm/2¾in long, on 7.5cm/3in stalks. Panicles of 10–30 irregular flower clusters, each of around six tubular flowers, appear in spring; the sepals are pink and white with slightly hairy margins, and the spoon-shaped, pointed petals are up to 2.5cm/1in long, white becoming fawn or pink. The arrow-shaped anthers are white, eventually becoming blue, and the pollen is noticeably blue.

Distribution: Western Australia.
Height and spread: Variable.
Habit and form: Twining shrub.
Leaf shape: Elliptic.
Pollinated: Insect.

Sweet Pittosporum

Native daphne, *Pittosporum undulatum*

The moist gullies in the forests of south-east Queensland to eastern Victoria are home to this tree with coarse, grey bark and glossy, green, elliptical, wavy-edged leaves. The small, white fragrant flowers appear abundantly at the branch tips in spring and early summer and in the autumn are followed by orange-tan berries, which persist for several months. Despite being native to Australia, this species has become an environmental weed in Tasmania, western Australia, western Victoria and South Australia, as well as in bushland around Sydney, chiefly because it has been favoured by habitat changes created by urban development.

Distribution: Eastern Australia.
Height and spread: 9–14m/30–45ft.
Habit and form: Evergreen tree.
Leaf shape: Ovate.
Pollinated: Insect.

Right: This tree forms an evergreen "mop" of foliage.

Far right: The brown woody seed capsules appear quite berry-like.

Identification: The laurel-like leaves, alternate to whorled, are 7.5–15cm/3–6in long, with pointed tips and distinctive wavy margins. The sweetly fragrant, tubular flowers are borne in terminal clusters from late spring to early summer; they are 12–20mm/½–¾in across with five creamy-white reflexed petals. The fruit is a dry, woody capsule, up to 12mm/½in in diameter, yellow, brown or orange, containing brown seeds with a sticky, resinous coating.

OTHER ROSE, PITTOSPORUM AND TREMANDRA SPECIES OF NOTE

Karo *Pittosporum crassifolium*
The karo or stiffleaf cheesewood is a small tree found along the edges of forests and streams in New Zealand's North Island and Kermadec Island in the south-west Pacific. It has a dense, almost columnar crown, and the undersides of the leathery leaves are covered with velvety felt. Umbels of deep red blooms make a striking display.

Finger Flower *Cheiranthera cyanea*
Found in the scrubby woodlands of south-east Australia, finger flower is named after the five stamens, which are positioned in a row. It has dense, linear foliage and despite being a small shrub has very large, striking blue flowers, which are specially adapted for pollination by bees.

Bluebell Creeper *Sollya fusiformis*
From western Australia, this low shrub or vine has slender stems set with narrow, mid-green, glossy leaves. In summer and autumn it displays clusters of little bell-shaped, pale mid-blue blossoms, followed by small, blue berries.

Rubus queenslandicus
This pinnate-leaved species of native Australian bramble is endemic to coastal ranges of north Queensland. The white, hairy, five-petalled flowers are followed by characteristic, red, conical, bramble fruits, which are dry in texture.

Pink Bells

Pink eye, *Tetratheca ciliata*

This widespread but uncommon Australian species, found in south Australia, Victoria and Tasmania, is restricted to coastal heaths and heathy woodland. It flowers in spring, when numerous, erect, slender stems sport a profusion of pink, four-petalled flowers with a darker central eye.

Identification: An understorey shrub with slender erect or spreading branches arising from a woody basal stock. The younger stems are clothed in fine short hairs, the older ones largely smooth. The rough-textured oval leaves, up to 12mm/½in long, grow in scattered groups of three or four, alternate to opposite or whorled. The flowers are four-parted, solitary, terminal or in the leaf axils, with purple or lilac petals up to 12mm/½in long. The fruit is a two-celled, flattened capsule.

Right: The erect or spreading branches arise from a woody base.

Distribution: Southern Australia.
Height and spread: 90cm/3ft.
Habit and form: Shrub.
Leaf shape: Ovate.
Pollinated: Insect.

Below: The four-petalled flowers are pink with a darker eye.

LEGUMES

Legumes form a significant component of nearly all terrestrial habitats, on all continents (except Antarctica), and are well represented in Australasia and the oceanic islands. They range from dwarf herbaceous perennials of alpine vegetation to massive trees in tropical forests with Australia being an especially rich source of these showy plants.

Yellow Kowhai

Sophora tetraptera

This small tree occurs naturally only on North Island, New Zealand, but is now widely cultivated throughout that country and can also be found in Chile. It is most commonly found growing along streams and forest margins, from East Cape to the Ruahine Range and from sea level up to 450m/1,500ft. It can reach 12m/40ft in height depending upon the altitude. In spring, birds feed on the nectar-rich flowers, which are followed by fruits that resemble strings of corky beads.

Top: the leaves are pinnate.

Above: The seedpod.

Distribution: North Island, New Zealand.
Height and spread: 4.5–12m/15–40ft.
Habit and form: Deciduous tree.
Leaf shape: Pinnate.
Pollinated: Bird.

Identification: A small to medium-size tree, occasionally shrubby, with spreading branches. The pinnate, mid-green leaves, 7.5–15cm/3–6in long, are much divided, with 20–40 oval to oblong leaflets. Racemes of four to ten greenish or golden-yellow, tubular, pendulous flowers, up to 6cm/2¼in long, appear in spring to summer. The brown pods of four-winged seeds are 6–7.5cm/2¼–3in long.

Left: This small, open-crowned tree varies considerably in height depending upon the altitude within which it grows.

Cockies' Tongue

Templetonia retusa

This fast-growing, evergreen shrub, native to South and Western Australia, gets its common name from its flowers, which allegedly resemble a cockatoo's tongue. It is frequently found growing on limestone, or sand or loam over limestone, mostly in coastal areas. The flowers appear in late summer, continuing until well into the winter, hence its popularity with birds at a time when other nectar sources are scarce.

Distribution: South and Western Australia.
Height and spread: 30cm–3m/1–10ft.
Habit and form: Evergreen shrub.
Leaf shape: Obovate.
Pollinated: Bird.

Identification: A spreading, much-branched shrub of variable height, it is frequently somewhat glaucous, with smooth, angled and grooved branches. The rounded, leathery leaves are grey-green, up to 4cm/1½in long, oval to wedge-shaped with a notched or blunt tip. Large red pea-like flowers are borne terminally or in the leaf axils in winter and spring, singly or in groups. They are up to 4cm/1½in long, with scale-like bracts and petals that are often darker at the tips. The oblong fruit may be up to 8cm/3¼in long, pale to dark brown.

Left: The pea-like flowers have a keel (the two lower petals) that allegedly resemble a cockatoo's tongue.

Left: This evergreen shrub varies in height and in some cases resembles a small tree.

Rusty Pods

Hovea longifolia

Distribution: Eastern Australia.
Height and spread: 3m/10ft.
Habit and form: Shrub.
Leaf shape: Linear.
Pollinated: Insect.

Right: Hovea longifolia is not well-known in cultivation, but when seen in the wild, forms an eye-catching specimen.

The most widespread and variable species in this genus is found in dry open forests in eastern Australia, extending from north Queensland to Victoria, especially on sandy soils. It is an erect understorey shrub with elongated, coarse-textured leaves, closely spaced on erect stems from where the rich violet flowers appear in small clusters in the leaf axils. They eventually give rise to short, inflated pods, covered with short rusty hairs: these split rapidly and shoot out the seeds for some distance upon ripening.

Identification: An upright shrub with erect, felted stems. The narrow leaves are glossy and leathery, dark green above and paler beneath, up to 7cm/2¾in long. In spring, bluish-purple pea flowers appear in clusters of two or three along the branchlets, with dark blue veins and a central yellow blotch; the calyx is covered with grey or red hairs. The globular or egg-shaped pod, covered with rust-coloured hairs, contains two hard-coated seeds.

Left: This upright shrub is quite variable across its range and is most noticeable when the flowers appear in spring.

OTHER LEGUMES OF NOTE

Holly Flame Pea *Chorizema ilicifolium*
Belonging to an endemic Australian genus of about 18 species, this is a small, spreading shrub with deeply lobed leaves with prickly teeth. The large pea flowers are bright red and orange, usually appearing in late winter and spring.

Climbing Wedge Pea
Gompholobium polymorphum
This variable plant from western Australia may occur as a slender, twining climber or a loose dwarf shrub. Its linear to oval leaves are variable in form and are a foil to the equally variable, large pinkish-red pea flowers that bloom in spring.

Coral Pea *Hardenbergia violacea*
Known as Australian sarsaparilla or native wisteria, this evergreen twining plant is a woody-stemmed species occurring in Victoria, Queensland, New South Wales, Tasmania and south Australia, in a variety of habitats from coast to mountains, usually in open forest or woodland and sometimes in heath. The flowers, which appear in winter and spring, are usually violet, but other colours are found.

Cape Arid Climber *Kennedia beckxiana*
This moderate to vigorous Australian climber has large trifoliate leaves and prominent scarlet, pea-shaped flowers with greenish-yellow blotches in spring to early summer.

Sturt's Desert Pea

Clianthus formosus

This short-lived species was adopted as the floral emblem of South Australia in 1961, although it mainly occurs in the dry central part of Australia and is named after Charles Sturt, who explored inland Australia in the 19th century. It is found in arid woodlands and on open plains, often as an ephemeral following heavy rain. It is one of Australia's most spectacular wild flowers: its large flag-shaped blooms are generally bright red but may be pure white to deep purple in some specimens.

Identification: A slow-growing, creeping plant, sometimes with a woody base, it may be annual or perennial. Most parts have a fine covering of silky hairs. The prostrate stems are long and thick, and the leaves, up to 18cm/7in long, are pinnate, with 9–21 oval, grey-green leaflets. The flowers are up to 7.5cm/3in long, with five or six held horizontally (appearing pendulous), on erect, thick-stalked racemes up to 30cm/12in tall. The scarlet flowers are up to 7.5cm/3in long, with five or six held horizontally on erect, thick-stalked racemes.

Distribution: Australia.
Height and spread: Variable.
Habit and form: Variable subshrub.
Leaf shape: Pinnate.
Pollinated: Insect.

Left: The red flowers have a deep red to black standard that protrudes and appears boss-like.

CABBAGE AND CAPER FAMILIES

The Brassicaceae, or cabbage family, are herbs or rarely subshrubs mostly found in temperate regions.
Australasia has only around 160 species, although New Zealand and other southern oceanic islands have
some rare and interesting species. Capparidaceae, the caper family, includes 45 genera and 675 species of
shrubs, herbs and trees, chiefly from warmer climates, many of which produce mustard oils.

Bush Passionfruit

Australian caper bush, *Capparis spinosa* var. *nummularia*

This small shrub is extremely widespread, and although the species is apparently of Mediterranean origin, a history of aboriginal use of the *nummularia* variety would indicate that this variety is indigenous to the Australian mainland. The plants grow spontaneously in rock crevices, thriving best in nutrient-poor, sharply drained, gravelly soils. The roots penetrate deeply into the earth and their salt-tolerance allows them to flourish along shores within sea-spray zones.

Identification: A sprawling, mounding shrub with arching red stems and dark green, semi-succulent oval or round leaves on short leaf stalks. Large, solitary flowers appear at almost any time of the year, often at night, disappearing in the heat of the day; they are borne from the leaf axils on stalks up to 7.5cm/3in long, and have pure white petals and numerous feathery white stamens. The green fruit ripens to yellow, usually off the bush and is an edible, elongated berry.

Distribution: Australia.
Height and spread: 90cm–2m x 3m/3–6 x 10ft.
Habit and form: Shrub.
Leaf shape: Elliptic.
Pollinated: Insect.

Far left and below left: The fruit is an elongated pod.

Right: This sprawling shrub commonly forms a mound in poor dry soils.

Kerguelen Island Cabbage

Pringlea antiscorbutica

This plant's common name is derived from its appearance and from the island of its discovery. Although most plants in the cabbage family are insect-pollinated, the Kerguelen Island cabbage has adapted to wind pollination (in the absence of winged insects on subantarctic islands) to exploit the almost continual winds in this region. The large, cabbage-like leaves contain a pale yellow, highly pungent essential oil that is rich in vitamin C, rendering the plant a useful dietary supplement against scurvy for early sailors. Despite its name it is also found elsewhere in the Southern Ocean, on the Crozet Archipelago and Marion Island.

Identification: A large rosette-forming, evergreen, herbaceous plant with smooth, spoon-shaped leaves with strong parallel veins, arising from stout, overground rhizomes extending 1.2m/4ft or more from the roots. The flowers are arranged on dense spikes, appearing axially from each rosette; they usually lack petals – although between one and four white, sometimes pink, petals may develop – and the stamens and thread-like stigma project from tiny sepals.

Right: The large cabbage-like rosettes give the plant its common name.

Distribution: Subantarctic, centred on Kerguelen Island.
Height and spread: Up to 45cm/18in across.
Habit and form: Herbaceous plant.
Leaf shape: Spathulate.
Pollinated: Wind.

Long-style Bittercress

Rorippa gigantea

Distribution: New Zealand.
Height and spread:
30–200cm/1–6½m.
Habit and form: Annual to perennial herb.
Leaf shape: Pinnatifid.
Pollinated: Insect.

This large cress-like plant grows in coastal regions mostly in New Zealand's North Island but is also known from an isolated population in the northeastern part of South Island. It is perfectly at home in salt spray on clifftops and coastal slopes, sometimes within active petrel colonies, around their burrow entrances but is rare in many places now due to grazing and exotic insect pests (particularly cabbage white butterfly). The large inflorescences support a multitude of tiny white flowers in spring and early summer.

Identification: This annual to perennial herb (depending on local growing conditions), grows 30–200cm/1–6½ft tall, arising from a stout taproot and one or more basal stems. The stems are erect to decumbent, slightly woody, purple-red when mature and angled. The leaves vary between yellow-green, dark green or purple-green, with margins that are entire or toothed and pinnatifid. The inflorescence is a complex, heavily branched raceme, appearing in spring to early summer. Each individual flower is tiny with white petals, 2–3mm/⅛–⅛in long. Fruits appear in summer, consisting of dark green to purple-green siliquae (specialized seedpods), with orange to red-brown seed, that is extremely sticky when fresh.

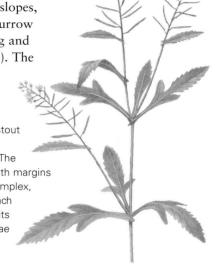

OTHER CABBAGE AND CAPER SPECIES OF NOTE

Notothlaspi australe
This species of penwiper, from New Zealand, can be found across a restricted range in mountain screes in the Torlesse Range of central South Island. It is similar to the other species from the island but sometimes forms dense colonies and has more rounded flowerheads.

Coastal Cress *Lepidium flexicaule*
This small, flat, creeping cress was once wide-spread in New Zealand, on bluffs, outcrops and among coastal turfs, but is now largely restricted to west and north-west South Island. The many racemes of small, white flowers, often hidden among foliage, appear in early summer.

Cook's Scurvy Grass *Lepidium oleraceum*
A bushy, aromatic, white-flowered herb, found in coastal areas and some offshore islands of New Zealand's South Island. It was abundant during the voyages of James Cook in the 18th century, and eaten to prevent scurvy. It is now scarce and endangered across its former range.

New Zealand Bittercress
Cardamine corymbosa
This tiny species of cress flowers all year but is mainly seen in autumn and winter. The tiny white flowers, which are self-pollinated, are followed by tiny explosive seedpods. The exceptional seeding ability of the plant has led to it becoming a troublesome weed in certain horticultural situations well outside its native range.

Penwiper Plant

Notothlaspi rosulatum

This curious little alpine herbaceous perennial, one of only two in this genus, is widespread on mountain screes at altitudes of around 800–1,800m/2,600–5,850ft in the Southern Alpine area of New Zealand's South Island. Its common name is derived from the structure of the plant, which allegedly looks like a 19th-century penwiper. The flat rosette of grey leaves is well camouflaged among the rocks, but when the large, conical flowerhead of fragrant, white flowers appears in summer it becomes quite conspicuous.

Distribution: South Island, New Zealand.
Height and spread:
7–25cm/2¾–10in.
Habit and form: Alpine herb.
Leaf shape: Spathulate.
Pollinated: Insect.

Identification: An erect, pyramidal, alpine herbaceous perennial with a long, central taproot. The fleshy, toothed, spoon-shaped leaves form a dense basal rosette or cushion, and are very numerous, overlapping, hairy at first, becoming more or less smooth. The large, white, four-petalled, fragrant flowers appear in summer, borne on a crowded pyramidal raceme.

GENTIAN, BELLFLOWER, TRIGGER PLANT AND GOODENIA FAMILIES

The Gentianaceae, or gentians, and the Campanulaceae, or bellflowers, are scarce in Australasia, though the gentians include some remarkable island endemics. Stylidiaceae, the trigger plant family, are small herbs, and Goodeniaceae, or goodenia, comprises sappy shrubs, herbs and trees; both thrive in Australia.

'Oha wai

Clermontia parviflora

This Hawaiian endemic is restricted to the wet forests of the Kohala Mountains and windward Mauna Kea and Mauna Loa, at heights of 120–1,450m/400–4750ft, where it can be found growing as a terrestrial shrub and as an epiphyte. It is one of the smaller-flowered *Clermontia* species, and is susceptible to browsing and habitat alteration by wild goats and pigs. If only epiphytic plants are found in a given area, it usually indicates that pigs are eating the vegetation there. This is one of 100 species of lobeliods, which make up about 10 per cent of Hawaii's native flora.

Identification: The bark is green when young, turning grey with age. The leaves, which are mainly clustered around the branch tips, are dark green above, paler below, with a purple midrib and stalk whose colour becomes less pronounced with age; developing leaves are often purple. The leaves are 6–18cm/2¼–7in long and 2–5cm/¾–2in wide, with finely toothed margins and elongated, pointed tips. The small flowers are green, purple or white on the outside, white or pale purple inside, tubular at the base, with narrow reflexed petals and projecting reproductive parts.

Distribution: Hawaii.
Height and spread: 3.5m/12ft.
Habit and form: Epiphytic or terrestrial shrub.
Leaf shape: Oblanceolate.
Pollinated: Bird.

Left: The plant has a candelabra-like habit, with branches usually arising from a single basal stem.

Far left: The yellow or orange berries have small ribs.

Pua'ala

Alula, Haha, *Brighamia rockii*

One of the most unusual plants of Hawaii, this plant, found only on the tall sea cliffs of the island Molokai, formerly grew on sunny, well-drained hillsides on all the four main islands. It is extremely rare today, however, with fewer than 100 plants growing in the wild. A strange plant that looks like a cabbage on a stick, it is a long-lived succulent, with a swollen base tapering toward a crowning rosette of fleshy leaves and yellow or white, trumpet-shaped flowers. It is presumed to be moth-pollinated although the moth is thought to have become extinct, so seed is not produced on wild plants.

Identification: The thickened, succulent stem, usually branching, tapers from the base and is distinctly purple during its juvenile stage. The shiny, leathery leaves are arranged in a rosette at the top of each branch; they are bright to dark green, 6–23cm/2¼–9in long and 5–15cm/2–6in across. The fragrant, trumpet-shaped, five-petalled, white flowers are clustered in groups of three to eight in the leaf axils, forming a dense rosette at the top of the stem in autumn.

Distribution: Molokai, Hawaii.
Height and spread: 5m/16ft.
Habit and form: Shrub.
Leaf shape: Obovate or spathulate.
Pollinated: Probably a moth (now extinct).

Far left: This strange plant looks a little like a cabbage on a stick.

Left: The large, white, trumpet-shaped flowers are fragrant and appear in the autumn.

Trigger Plant

Stylidium spathulatum

Distribution: Western Australia.
Height and spread: 25cm/10in.
Habit and form: Herbaceous perennial.
Leaf shape: Obovate.
Pollinated: Insect.

The curious trigger plants are so named because of the rapid flick of the column when touched by a visiting insect. This column protrudes from the flower and bears the stamens and stigma. In the "cocked" position it is kinked at the base and sticks out to one side between two of the petals. When an insect attempts to take nectar from the flower, the sensitive base, irritated by its touch, straightens instantaneously and swings the stamens and stigma through an arc, hitting the animal and showering it with pollen. As the flower ages the stamens shrivel, but the stigma protrudes from the end of the column, ready to be brushed by insects already covered in pollen.

Identification: Oblong to spoon-shaped leaves, covered with green, yellow or brown glandular hairs, form a basal rosette. The flowers are pale yellow, borne in loose, unbranched racemes on a leafless stem 15–50cm/6–20in tall. The calyx has five lobes, more or less united into two lips; the corolla lobes are irregular, with four arranged in two pairs and the labellum much smaller and turned, or nearly as long and curved upward; the column is elongated and bent down, elastic.

Left: The flower is the easiest means of identifying trigger plants.

Right: All Stylidium *species have four petals.*

OTHER GENTIAN, BELLFLOWER AND TRIGGER PLANTS OF NOTE

'Oha Wai Nui *Clermontia arborescens*

'Oha wai nui is endemic to Maui, where it occurs in mesic (moist) to wet forest from 520–1,850m/ 1,700–6,000ft. Its fleshy, claw-shaped, strongly arched flowers are among the largest of the genus and are pale green with purple columns.

Thick-leaved Trigger Plant

Stylidium crassifolium

The fleshy leaves that cluster about the base of the flower stem give rise to this plant's common name. It grows to 60cm/2ft. It comes from western Australia, where it is found near wet flushes and drying creek beds, especially following bushfires.

Cunningham's Snow-gentian

Chionogentias cunninghamii

Naturally found in swamps and wet heath in New South Wales, this tall gentian has white flowers. Australian gentians of this genus mostly occur in the alpine or subalpine zone, although this species mainly occurs at lower altitudes.

Boomerang Trigger Plant

Stylidium breviscapum

This creeping herbaceous perennial from western Australia grows to 20cm/8in high and is curiously elevated up to 7cm/2¾in above the soil by wiry, black, stilt roots. The flowers are white with red markings, appearing from early spring to summer.

Blue Leschenaultia

Leschenaultia biloba

Aboriginal people are said to have called blue leschenaultia, which is native to the sand hills of western Australia, "the floor of the sky", because the ground where it grows is carpeted with its blue flowers. In many areas the plant adopts a suckering habit, enabling it to spread over a wide area and resulting in massed spring displays. Arguably one of the most beautiful Australian species, its flower is designed to attract bees. It has a blue "landing platform" with a white centre that helps guide the bee to the nectar at the base of the tubular petals. To reach the nectar the bee must either pick up or deposit pollen.

Identification: A diffuse, small, sprawling to climbing, semi-woody, evergreen perennial or subshrub. It has tiny, narrow, heath-like, soft grey-green leaves 12mm/ ½in long. The flowers, up to 2.5cm/1in across, appear from late winter to late spring, with five pointed lobes with distinctive large corolla wings, veined with parallel, transverse lines. They range from deep purplish-blue through sky-blue to pale blue.

Distribution: Western Australia.
Height and spread: 50cm/20in; indefinite spread.
Habit and form: Evergreen perennial.
Leaf shape: Narrow.
Pollinated: Insect.

Right: The bright blue flowers open from greenish buds.

Below: The plant commonly forms a heath-like sprawling shrub.

GERANIUM, PORTULACA AND AMARANTH FAMILIES

The Geraniaceae, or geraniums, are a varied family usually featuring five-petalled flowers and a beaked fruit that often disperses the seed explosively. The Portulacaceae (portulacas) comprise mainly herbaceous perennials; the Amaranthaceae (amaranths) are mostly herbs but also rarely shrubs or small trees.

Broad-leaf Parakeelya

Rock purslane, *Calandrinia balonensis*

This fleshy herb, with flowers that open quickly in response to sunshine, belongs to a genus of around 150 species, which occur in Australia and from Canada to Chile. *C. balonensis* is named after the Balonne River in Queensland, where it was first collected, and is one of approximately 30 Australian species. It grows as an annual or perennial in arid areas of southern Australia and the Northern Territory, often around salt lakes, and its bright, shiny, red flowers, amid flattened, succulent, finger-length leaves, often carpet large areas in spring.

Right: This low-growing, fleshy herb spreads from woody branches near the base.

Identification: A low-growing, spreading or trailing herbaceous perennial, with the older branches becoming woody near the base. The leaves are alternate, fleshy and narrow, with a very pronounced, somewhat flattened midrib. The long-lasting, five-petalled flowers, up to 2.5cm/1in across, are borne from the leaf axils. They have two persistent sepals, vibrant pinky-red petals with paler, often white, bases and yellow centres with numerous filaments.

Distribution: Australia.
Height and spread: 15–40cm/6–16in.
Habit and form: Herbaceous perennial.
Leaf shape: Narrow.
Pollinated: Insect.

Pink Mulla Mulla

Lamb's tail, *Ptilotus exaltatus*

This ephemeral plant inhabits a wide range of habitats stretching across the mainland from the north-west of Australia. The flowers are borne on candelabra-like branches, and the time of year in which they appear depends largely upon seasonal rainfall patterns: in arid areas they are usually most abundant following good rains. It is a common and widespread plant, with specimens from the westernmost regions being generally taller with longer inflorescences and less hairy than their eastern counterparts.

Identification: A stout, erect, perennial with hairless stems, branched or unbranched, growing from woody rhizomes. The thick, wavy-edged leaves, up to 10cm/4in long, are bright blue-green tinged red, forming a rosette at the base of the plant. The pink, fluffy flowers appear on tall stems in conical spikes, becoming cylindrical with age, up to 15cm/6in long and 5cm/2in wide.

Far left: The stems are stout and erect.

Distribution: North-west Australia.
Height and spread: 90cm/3ft.
Habit and form: Erect perennial.
Leaf shape: Oblong-lanceolate.
Pollinated: Insect.

Left: The flowers of pink mulla mulla often form striking displays following rains.

Southern Stork's Bill

Pelargonium australe

This is a widespread and variable plant that is generally found growing in sand dunes near the coast, between rocky outcrops, and inland, sometimes at higher elevations in subalpine regions. It often flowers over a long period, and the leaves may take on orange or even darker tones in the autumn. Plants collected in Tasmania are smaller in all parts, with dark green leaves and red leaf stalks and although they resemble the mainland species in most other respects some botanists recognize some populations to be separate subspecies.

Left: This straggling shrubby plant varies considerably in height and colour across its native range.

Distribution: South-eastern Australia, Tasmania, and New Zealand.
Height and spread: 30cm/1ft.
Habit and form: Subshrub.
Leaf shape: Rounded.
Pollinated: Insect.

Identification: A straggling, short-stemmed, softly hairy, shrubby, erect, low-growing perennial shrub. The heart-shaped, faintly aromatic leaves are up to 10cm/4in in diameter, rounded and shallowly lobed, and are very soft, being covered with thick, soft hairs. Each flowering stem bears a compact umbel of 5–25 flowers, which vary in colour from white to pale blush to pink, with dark red spots and feathering, appearing in spring or summer.

OTHER GERANIUM, PORTULACA AND AMARANTH SPECIES OF NOTE

Pussy Tails *Ptilotus spathulatus*
This low-growing Australian perennial has numerous stems arising from a stout rhizome. The rounded or spoon-shaped, fleshy leaves are held basally, and the cylindrical flower spikes emerge over a long period between winter and summer, bearing yellow, green or golden flowers, either solitary or clustered.

Rose-tipped Mulla Mulla *Ptilotus manglesii* This Australian perennial sometimes lasts only as an annual, with stems that trail along the ground a little before ascending at the tips. The long, rounded leaves have stems near the base of the plant, becoming stalkless near the top. The round flower spikes are covered with shaggy white hairs, among which the pink to violet-purple flowers nestle in summer.

Geranium homeanum
This widespread plant is found in Java, Timor, Samoa, New Zealand and the east coastal states of Australia. It is commonly found in grassland, thin forests and on roadsides. The prostrate, often hairy stems support lobed leaves with large teeth, and the small, white to pale pink flowers appear from late spring to late summer.

Small storksbill *Erodium angustilobum*
Found from Queensland to south Australia, this annual has narrow, basal leaves, which are deeply seven-lobed. In summer it sports numerous blue to pinkish flowers on ascending stems that reach 30cm/12in.

Purslane

Pigweed, *Portulaca oleracea*

Purslane is a species that grows worldwide and, although generally regarded as a weed in many parts of Australia, it is a native of that continent. It is found throughout Australia except in Tasmania. In inland areas dense colonies of the plant appear after rain. It is edible and has long been used as a vegetable, as a substitute for spinach, or as a salad leaf.

Identification: A succulent, prostrate annual herb with smooth, reddish-brown stems and alternate, oval, succulent leaves, 2.5cm/1in long, clustered at the stem joints and ends. The yellow flowers, 6mm/¼in across with five two- or three-lobed petals, occur in the leaf axils; they appear in late spring and continue into mid-autumn, each opening singly at the centre of a leaf cluster for only a few hours on sunny mornings. The seeds are contained in a pod.

Right: The tiny, black seeds are contained in a pod, the top of which falls off once the seeds are ripe.

Distribution: Cosmopolitan in warm areas.
Height and spread: 40cm/16in.
Habit and form: Succulent herb.
Leaf shape: Obovate.
Pollinated: Insect.

OLEANDER AND BRAZIL NUT FAMILIES

The Apocynaceae (oleanders or dogbane family) are distributed mainly in the tropics and subtropics, though some perennial herbs thrive in temperate regions. Plants of this family may have milky sap and are often poisonous. The Lecythidaceae (Brazil nuts) are woody plants native to tropical climates. The Brazil nut is the most well known and important species from this family.

Indian Oak

Freshwater mangrove, *Barringtonia acutangula*

Indian oak grows in coastal areas in the tropics, or on seasonally inundated land by lagoons, creeks and riverbanks. In areas prone to seasonal dry periods, it may be partially deciduous. In Australia it is found mainly in the Northern Territory and is striking when in flower due to its handsome foliage and large pendulous sprays of pink or white, fluffy, scented flowers, which open in the evening and fall the following morning.

Far right: Indian oak is a small flowering tree.

Identification: The leaves, crowded at the ends of the branches, are up to 15cm/6in long, lance-shaped to oval, smooth, finely toothed, with a midrib prominent on both sides. Terminal, pendulous racemes bear up to 75 flowers, ranging in colour from dark red to white, with four petals, stamens in three whorls fused at the base, and filaments protruding to 2cm/¾in. The fruit is single-seeded, fleshy, tapering at either end, up to 6cm/2¼in long.

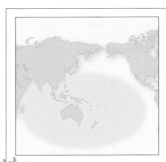

Distribution: Indo-Pacific region.
Height and spread: 13m/42ft.
Habit and form: Shrub or small tree.
Leaf shape: Oblanceolate.
Pollinated: Uncertain, possibly bat or moth.

Bloodhorn

Mangrove ochrosia, *Ochrosia elliptica*

This large shrub or small spreading tree can be found along northern and central coastal Queensland, on Lord Howe Island and parts of Melanesia in fore-dune vine thickets immediately behind the mangroves. The small, yellow or white flowers are sweetly fragrant and occur in small clusters between mid-spring and late summer and are followed by pairs of striking, red fruits, which resemble red horns or elongated tomatoes. These often persist on the tree for a considerable time. Unfortunately, despite their appearance, the fruit are poisonous, and plants also bleed copious amounts of poisonous white sap when wounded, making it best to avoid contact with this tree.

Identification: A large evergreen shrub or small, spreading tree with stout, green young branches. The leaves are glossy, leathery, dark green, elliptic to oblong or oval, with smooth, wavy edges, up to 20cm/8in long and 8cm/3¼in wide, occurring in whorls of three or four. The flowers appear in axillary clusters and are fragrant, small and yellow or white. The showy, oval fruits, 5cm/2in long, are borne in pairs and are persistent on the tree.

Distribution: Australia, Melanesia.
Height and spread: 5–9m/16–30ft.
Habit and form: Large shrub or small tree.
Leaf shape: Elliptic to oblong.
Pollinated: Insect.

Left: This evergreen tree has a dense, spreading crown and is most noticeable when the bright red fruits ripen.

OTHER OLEANDER, BRAZIL NUT AND EUCALYPTUS SPECIES

Kalalau *Pteralyxia kauaiensis*
This long-lived small tree has shiny, dark green leaves that hide the small, greenish, tubular flowers. It is one of just two members of an endemic Hawaiian genus within Apocynaceae, growing in the Wahiawa Mountains in the southern portion of Kauai.

Kaulu *Pteralyxia macrocarpa*
The kaulu is the only other member of this rare Hawaiian genus and is a small tree found in valleys and slopes in diverse mesic forest on the island of Oahu. Its shiny, green leaves almost hide the yellowish, tubular flowers. It is rare, with 500 or so in the wild.

Water Gum *Tristania neriifolia*
A large shrub that may become a small tree, the water gum is found along the central coast and adjacent ranges of New South Wales, along the banks of streams. It has narrow leaves with conspicuous oil glands. The yellow, star-shaped flowers occur in summer, usually in groups of three to six. It is the only species in the genus.

Scarlet Kunzea *Kunzea baxteri*
This erect shrub from the south coastal areas of Western Australia has grey-green, oblong leaves and large, crimson flower clusters, which are arranged in bottlebrush form and are very profuse and conspicuous in spring and early summer. The plant is related to the bottlebrushes, *Callistemon* species, and also bears a similarity to *Melaleuca* and *Leptospermum* species.

Falaga

Barringtonia samoensis

This shrub or small tree occurs in coastal areas or on seasonally inundated land by lagoons, creeks and riverbanks, from south-east Celebes to Micronesia, New Guinea and Polynesia. It bears spectacular pendulous spikes at the branch tips that may contain 150 or more individual, scented flowers of red or white, each with numerous long golden-yellow anthers and a single, persistent, red stigma.

Identification: The leaves, up to 90cm/3ft long with smooth margins or rounded teeth, are crowded at the ends of the branches, spirally arranged, with a midrib prominent on both sides. The flowers are borne in pendulous racemes up to 55cm/22in long, which may be terminal or sprout directly from the branches. They have four convex, white or red petals and numerous protruding yellow stamens, fused at the base in three to eight whorls. The ribbed fruit is single-seeded and fleshy, up to 7cm/2¾in long with a tapering base.

Distribution: Micronesia, New Guinea and Polynesia.
Height and spread: 12m/40ft.
Habit and form: Shrub or small tree.
Leaf shape: Obovate.
Pollinated: Insect.

Left: The spectacular flower spikes are borne at the branch tips and may contain 150 flowers.

Cocky Apple

Billy goat plum, *Planchonia careya*

This is a common, widespread small tree or spreading shrub found across much of northern tropical Australia and down the east coast to Fraser Island, most commonly in open forests and woodlands. It prefers moist places, such as the edges of floodplains and coastal monsoon forests, and flowers from spring to mid-autumn. It is related to the freshwater mangroves, *Barringtonia* species. It is night-flowering: the flowers open at dusk and persist only until the sun shines the following day.

Distribution: Tropical northern Australia.
Height and spread: 4–10m/13–33ft.
Habit and form: Small tree or spreading shrub.
Leaf shape: Ovate or spathulate.
Pollinated: Bat.

Above: Each of the large, fleshy flowers persists for just one night.

Far right: The fruit is green, egg-shaped and smooth.

Identification: The species is briefly deciduous in the dry season. The bark is grey, rough, slightly corky and fissured. The leaves are oval or spoon-shaped with rounded teeth on the margins, tapering to the base and up to 10cm/4in long. They are softly leathery, shiny, light green above, dull beneath, turning rusty-orange before falling. The large, fleshy flowers are white, grading to pink inside towards the base, with numerous pink-and-white stamens, 5cm/2in long, fused together into a tube at their bases. The flowers are borne only at night, the whole staminal bundle falling off as a single unit in the morning.

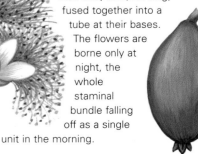

MYRTLE, EVENING PRIMROSE AND DAPHNE FAMILIES

The Myrtaceae, myrtle family, are trees and shrubs found in the warm-temperate regions of Australia. The family dominates the hardwood forests across the continent. The evening primrose family, Onagraceae, has a restricted distribution although the daphne family, Thymelaeaceae, is much more widespread.

Shining Copper Cups

Pileanthus rubronitidus

This small shrub is one species in a small genus restricted to Western Australia. Shining copper cups is found only between Kalbarri and west of Northampton, growing on grey sand over sandstone, or white sand, in heath or shrubland colonized by the sceptre banksia, *Banksia sceptum*, although isolated colonies have been reported from Mount Magnet. The orange-red flowers appear between early and late spring, although it is the conspicuous, cup-like calyces, persisting long after flowering, that give rise to the plant's common name.

Identification: A small, branching evergreen shrub with very narrow, three-sided, smooth leaves, up to 12mm/½in long, with prominent oil glands. The flowers appear in clusters around the upper leaf axils in spring, initially enclosed in a one-leaf bract; they are very distinctively red-orange, with ten sepals and five rounded petals, on a slender stem 12–25mm/½–1in long.

Distribution: Western Australia.
Height and spread: 90cm/3ft.
Habit and form: Shrub.
Leaf shape: Linear.
Pollinated: Insect.

Left: Shining copper cups forms a small open bush.

New Zealand Tea Tree

Manuka, *Leptospermum scoparium*

This shrub occurs widely throughout lowland to subalpine areas and in many habitats, chiefly in New Zealand, where it is considered to be endemic, although some botanists claim that it is also a native species of Tasmania, New South Wales and Victoria, Australia. It is by far the commonest shrubland constituent and has increased greatly under the influence of human settlement. The English common name is derived from the fact that early white settlers made infusions of tea from the leaves, which are aromatic. The white blooms appear in spring and early summer, often so profusely that it resembles snow.

Identification: A bushy, evergreen shrub ranging in size from a creeping plant to a small tree, although it is seldom more than 4m/13ft high. It is adaptable and extremely variable in leaf size and shape, flower and leaf colour, branching habit and foliage density, as well as oil content and aroma. Differences occur in individual plants, within and among populations, genetically and with season, soil and other variables. The bark sheds in long papery strips. The thick leaves are narrow and less than 15mm/⅝in long, with sharp pointed tips, hard and leathery, with aromatic scent glands beneath, variable in colour from very pale green to dark brown; younger shrubs have softer, paler leaves. Showy, mostly white, sometimes pink or reddish flowers, 1.5cm/⅝in across, are borne profusely in spring.

Distribution: New Zealand, eastern Australia.
Height and spread: 4–6m/13–20ft.
Habit and form: Shrub or small tree.
Leaf shape: Narrow.
Pollinated: Insect.

Above left: The fruits are woody capsules containing numerous small, thin seeds.

Left: This variable shrub can have a creeping habit or be almost tree-like.

Mottlecah

Rose of the west, *Eucalyptus macrocarpa* subsp. *macrocarpa*

Distribution: Western Australia.
Height and spread: Up to 5m/16ft.
Habit and form: Mallee shrub.
Leaf shape: Ovate.
Pollinated: Insect.

This species of eucalyptus is distinctive in having a growth habit in which several woody stems arise separately from a lignotuber, or starchy swelling on underground stems or roots – a form known as a "mallee". It is chiefly found on open sandy heath in Western Australia. It is quite variable in form, with two subspecies often reported: the subspecies *elachantha* is restricted in occurrence and differs from the common form in having smaller leaves and lower stature.

Right: The large gumnuts contain many tiny seeds.

Identification: A spreading or sprawling mallee with smooth bark throughout, grey over salmon-pink. The glaucous, silvery grey-green leaves are opposite, 5–12.5cm/2–5in long, stalkless and oval, while the young leaves are almost circular. Spectacular large flowers, up to 10cm/4in across, appear from early spring to midsummer, with a mass of stamens that are usually red, occasionally pinky-red or cream. The very large, shallowly hemispherical "gumnuts" that follow them have a powdery grey covering.

Far left: This medium to large shrub grows from an underground stem that protects it from fires.

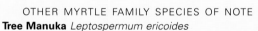

OTHER MYRTLE FAMILY SPECIES OF NOTE

Tree Manuka *Leptospermum ericoides*
This large shrub or small tree can reach 15m/50ft high. It has loose, peeling bark and small, pointed, aromatic leaves. The small, white, five-petalled flowers cover mature specimens in spring and early summer with a mass of blossom. It is abundant in lowland and mountain forests throughout New Zealand.

Lutulutu *Eugenia gracilipes*
This graceful tree possesses delicate foliage and drooping branches, which bear terminal slender racemes of three to seven pale yellow or pink-tinged flowers. It is found only in the Fiji islands. Related species include *Sygyzium malaccensis*, the malay apple, which has deep purple, crimson or even white flowers and reddish fruits, much valued locally for eating.

Pohutukawa *Metrosideros excelsa*
The New Zealand Christmas tree gains its name from its time of flowering and forms a wide-spreading tree with round, leathery, dark green leaves and large flowers most noted for their spectacular sprays of red stamens. Its natural distribution is restricted to the coastal forest in the North Island.

Rata *Metrosideros robusta*
The rata is an inhabitant of the forests of New Zealand's North Island but can also be found on Three Knights Island and western South Island. It forms a large tree, with dull red flowers appearing in summer. The plant often begins life as an epiphyte, perching in another tree. In time, roots are sent down to the ground, and the *Metrosideros* takes over.

Copper Cups

Pileanthus peduncularis

This small rounded shrub, found only on the south-western Australian sand plains, is probably the best-known member of the genus. It is often encountered among sand dunes north of Perth, although its distribution is scattered. It is a spectacular sight in spring with its unusual, large, copper-orange flowers, which occur towards the ends of the branches and from the leaf axils in a massed display. The conspicuous, cup-like calyces often persist for a long time after flowering.

Identification: Small, branching evergreen shrub with very narrow, three-sided, smooth leaves up to 4mm/⅛in long, with prominent oil glands. The flowers appear in clusters toward the ends of the branches and from the leaf axils, initially enclosed in a one-leaf bract; they are up to 2.5cm/1in across, copper-orange, sometimes red, with ten sepals and five rounded petals, on a slender stem 12–25mm/½–1in long.

Distribution: South-western Australia.
Height and spread: 90cm/3ft.
Habit and form: Shrub.
Leaf shape: Linear.
Pollinated: Insect.

Above: The cup-like calyces often persist well after flowering.

Below: The plant forms a low, branching, rounded shrub on sandy soils.

Bottlebrush

Callistemon brachyandrus

This large bushy shrub is found growing naturally in western New South Wales, Victoria and South Australia. It is one of the later flowering bottlebrushes and flowers during the summer, often after others of the genus have finished. Like so many of Australia's attractive native plants, the inflorescences of *Callistemon* are composed of a large number of small flowers grouped together. The flower arrangement closely resembles a bottle-cleaning brush, hence the common name. The small red brushes cover the branches, and the masses of stamens are dark red with yellow anthers, giving the flowers the appearance of being dusted with gold.

Above and below right: The bush forms a dense shrub with flowers appearing at the branch tips.

Distribution: South-eastern Australia.
Height and spread: 4m/13ft.
Habit and form: Shrub.
Leaf shape: Linear.
Pollinated: Insect.

Identification: A dense, small to tall shrub. The prolific young shoots are grey, silky, soft and hairy, distinct from the mature needle-like leaves, which are up to 4cm/1½in long, stiff and sharp-pointed, pungent, with undersides typically dotted with oil glands. The flowers are borne in loose spikes up to 8cm/3¼in long, appearing in mid- to late summer; the five small, green petals and sepals, together with the pistils, are barely noticeable among the showy, orange-red stamens, with gold anthers.

Lesser Bottlebrush

Fiery bottlebrush, *Callistemon phoeniceus*

Despite its common name, this plant is actually a medium-sized shrub that is widespread in south-west Western Australia. It is one of only two species that occur there. It naturally grows in depressions and along watercourses extending from the Swan River to the Murchison River, with its eastern limits in the Norseman area.

Below right: This medium-sized shrub often resembles a small pendulous tree.

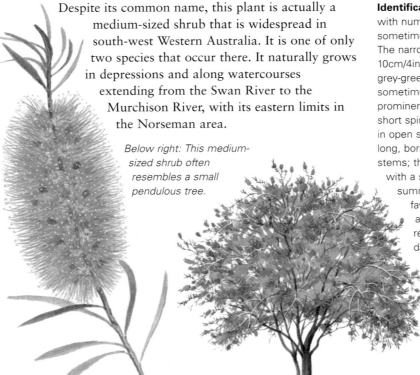

Identification: A medium shrub with numerous branches, sometimes slightly pendulous. The narrow leaves are up to 10cm/4in long, blue-green to grey-green, thick, rigid, sometimes twisted, with a prominent midrib, tipped with a short spine. The flowers grow in open spikes 10–15cm/4–6in long, borne terminally on slender stems; they appear in late spring, with a second flowering in late summer if conditions are favourable. The stamens are a bright rich red, usually with darker anthers.

Right: The fluffy red flowerheads resemble bottle-cleaning brushes and give rise to the common name.

Distribution: Western Australia.
Height and spread: 3m/10ft.
Habit and form: Shrub.
Leaf shape: Linear-lanceolate.
Pollinated: Insect.

Arakura

Scarlet rata, *Metrosideros fulgens*

This plant is one of a number of rata vines found in New Zealand. Unlike *M. robusta* however, which begins as a vine and often grows into a tree, the scarlet rata needs support throughout its life. It commonly flowers from late summer into autumn, when it can be seen scrambling and twining over logs and up trees, and is considered an early sign that winter is approaching.

Distribution: New Zealand.
Height and spread: 10m/33ft or more.
Habit and form: Liana.
Leaf shape: Elliptic-oblong.
Pollinated: Insect.

Left: The plant is a liana and needs the support of another tree to reach its full height.

Identification: A liana with aromatic bark, separating in flakes, and smooth leaves up to 7.5cm/3in long, opposite, simple, pinnately veined and dotted with glands, on stout leaf stalks. The flowers are in terminal clusters, with oblong sepals, round orange-red petals and a mass of scarlet stamens up to 2.5cm/1in long. The fruit is a leathery capsule.

Right: The small flowers are given added prominence by the mass of scarlet stamens.

OTHER MYRTLE FAMILY SPECIES OF NOTE

Alpine Bottlebrush *Callistemon pityoides*
The alpine bottlebrush forms dense thickets at altitudes of 2,000m/6,500ft or more, being found most commonly in and around sphagnum bogs and swamps, and along watercourses in eastern Australia. The colourful bracts that surround the developing buds first become evident in early spring, opening to reveal yellow flowers.

Crimson Bottlebrush *Callistemon citrinus*
From the east coast of Australia, this is an upright shrub with narrow, lance-shaped, leathery leaves with a distinctly citrus aroma (hence the specific name). The plump, bright red, bottlebrush-shaped flowers, composed mostly of stamens, bloom throughout the hot weather. The bark is rough and light brown.

Regelia cymbifolia
Occurring in a restricted area in south-west Western Australia in sandplain or woodland, this is a bushy, erect, many-branched shrub up to 1.8m/6ft tall. It has oval leaves and deep pink to purple flowers produced in small, terminal clusters in spring. The seeds are retained within the capsules until a fire prompts their release.

Gillham's Bell *Darwinia oxylepis*
This is a small shrub that may reach 1.5m/5ft, with narrow, recurved leaves. The small flowers are enclosed within large, deep red bracts with a characteristic bell shape, on the branch tips in spring.

Cranbrook Bell

Darwinia meeboldii

One of several species of *Darwinia* from south-western Australia, known collectively as "mountain bells", this plant is found in moist, peaty soils in the Stirling Ranges, although it is now rare. It is an erect, spindly, small to medium-sized shrub that bears clusters of around eight small flowers enclosed within large bracts. These give the inflorescence its characteristic bell shape.

Identification: The narrow, aromatic leaves are alternately paired, triangular in section, up to 1cm/⅜in long with prominent oil glands. Flowers appear from early to late spring, prominently displayed on the ends of the branches: small, white to red tubular flowers appear in groups of about eight enclosed within leafy, bell-shaped bracts, usually white with bright red tips, more rarely red or green.

Far right: The plant forms an erect, spindly, medium-sized shrub that is clothed with flowers in the spring.

Distribution: South-western Australia.
Height and spread: Variable.
Habit and form: Dwarf to medium shrub.
Leaf shape: Linear.
Pollinated: Insect.

Chenille Honey Myrtle

Melaleuca huegelii subsp. *huegelii*

This flowering shrub, native to south-western coastal districts of Western Australia, is unusual in that it flowers during the summer. Two subspecies are currently recognized, *huegelii* and *pristicensis*, the latter distinguished by its mauve to pink flowers held in narrow spikes. Both are medium to large shrubs, found on limestone cliffs, coastal plains and dunes. The leaves are very small and crowded against the stems in a scale-like manner, and these are covered with small oil glands. The long whip-like branches make this a highly distinctive plant.

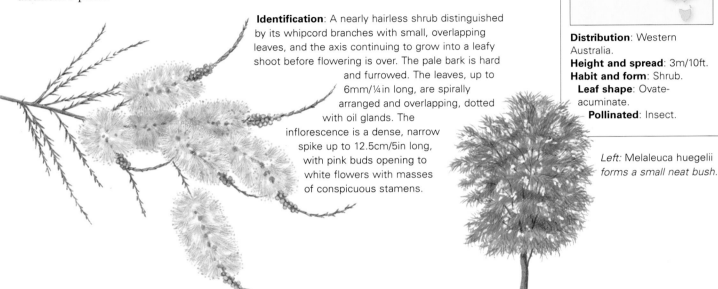

Identification: A nearly hairless shrub distinguished by its whipcord branches with small, overlapping leaves, and the axis continuing to grow into a leafy shoot before flowering is over. The pale bark is hard and furrowed. The leaves, up to 6mm/¼in long, are spirally arranged and overlapping, dotted with oil glands. The inflorescence is a dense, narrow spike up to 12.5cm/5in long, with pink buds opening to white flowers with masses of conspicuous stamens.

Distribution: Western Australia.
Height and spread: 3m/10ft.
Habit and form: Shrub.
Leaf shape: Ovate-acuminate.
Pollinated: Insect.

Left: Melaleuca huegelii forms a small neat bush.

Scarlet Honey Myrtle

Melaleuca fulgens

This well-known plant, from south-west Western Australia, north-west South Australia and the south-west of the Northern Territory, is common in cultivation in both its usual red-flowered form and in several other colours. The leaves and branches emit an aromatic fragrance when bruised. It occurs in various habitats, most commonly in rocky granite areas, and blooms in spring, with a typical bottlebrush form to the flowers. Birds, particularly honeyeaters searching for nectar, are attracted to the shrub when it is in flower.

Identification: The branches are smooth except for the young felted shoots, and the narrow, grey-green leaves, up to 3cm/1¼in long, are borne in alternate pairs on very short or no stalks. The inflorescence is a spike of 6–20 flowers, usually with the axis growing on into a leafy shoot; the numerous, conspicuous stamens, much longer than the petals, are scarlet or deep pink (rarely white). The urn-shaped fruit has a rough, wrinkled, almost papery texture.

Distribution: Western Australia.
Height and spread: 2.5m/8ft.
Habit and form: Shrub.
Leaf shape: Elliptic.
Pollinated: Bird.

Left: Scarlet honey myrtle forms a loose spreading shrub that is highly visible when in flower.

Fuchsia procumbens

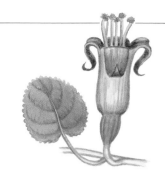

Distribution: North Island, New Zealand.
Height and spread: Variable.
Habit and form: Prostrate shrub.
Leaf shape: Suborbicular.
Pollinated: Insect.

Originating in North Island, New Zealand, this small shrubby plant grows in rocky, sandy or gravelly places near the sea, in areas that can occasionally be flooded by exceptionally high tides, where it may cover substantial areas. Due to the destruction of its natural habit, it is now an endangered species in the wild. It is prostrate in growth, with slender, trailing stems, small, heart-shaped leaves and distinctive, though rather diminutive, erect flowers.

Identification: Slender, branched, prostrate shrub with long, trailing shoots and alternate, round or heart-shaped leaves, 6–20mm/ ¼–¾in across, borne on thin stalks. The erect flowers, up to 20mm/¾in long, have a greenish-yellow tube that is red at the base, and purple-tipped, sharply reflexed green sepals and no true petals; the stamens bear bright blue pollen. The attractive seedpods are about 2cm/¾in long. They ripen from green to bright crimson, covered with a light bloom, and are long-lasting.

Above: The tiny orange flowers have strongly reflexed sepals and no true petals.

OTHER MYRTLE FAMILY SPECIES OF NOTE

Kotukutuku *Fuchsia excorticata*
The largest fuchsia in the world, growing in Central South America and New Zealand, particularly on North Island, where it is common in lowland to lower montane forest, especially along margins and in damp valleys. The solitary, red, pendulous flowers have blue pollen and the dark, egg-shaped fruit is relished by the Maoris and known as konini.

New Zealand Daphne *Pimelia prostrata*
This variable, low shrub is found in dry places in New Zealand where it may variously adopt a wide-spreading or tufted habit. The small, silky-downy white flowers are fragrant and appear in small crowded heads of between three and ten, on short side shoots near the ends of the branches, usually in spring or early summer.

Rosy Paperbark *Melaleuca diosmatifolia*
The rosy paperbark of eastern Australia is most commonly found in woodland and open forest, often in areas subject to inundation. It is a small shrub with narrow leaves ending in a small point. The pale to deep mauve flowers are usually seen in spring and early summer and occur in bottlebrush-type spikes on short branches.

Scarlet Feathers *Verticordia grandis*
A showy small shrub, found in woodlands and sandy heaths in south-western Australia. It has small, stem-clasping, rounded, grey-green leaves. Throughout the year it bears bright red, five-petalled flowers, each with a long, protruding style. The popularity of this species for floral arrangements has resulted in over-picking from the wild in some areas across its range.

Rice Flower

Pimelia ferruginea

This small to medium-sized, evergreen, woody shrub is one of around 80 species of so-called rice flowers, found throughout Australia and New Zealand, which are related to the European and Asian genus *Daphne*. The flowers are produced mainly in spring but can appear at any time, in dense heads borne at the tips of the branches.

Distribution: Australia and New Zealand.
Height and spread: 1.8m/6ft.
Habit and form: Evergreen shrub.
Leaf shape: Ovate or oblong.
Pollinated: Insect.

Identification: An erect, evergreen shrub with opposite, crowded leaves up to 12mm/½in long, shiny and smooth above, often hairy beneath, with rolled margins. Almost spherical flowerheads, up to 4cm/1½in across, appear in late spring to early summer, held at the ends of branchlets and surrounded by leaf-like pink or red bracts. The tubular, four-petalled flowers are rose-pink with a paler centre.

Right: Rice flower forms a medium-sized shrub with crowded leafy stems.

PASSIONFLOWER, VIOLET AND SAXIFRAGE FAMILIES

The Passifloraceae (passionflowers) are tropical climbers and woody shrubs. Members of the Violaceae, the violet family, are widely distributed with species being herbaceous trees or shrubs. The Saxifragaceae, or saxifrage family, includes herbaceous perennials and deciduous shrubs typically in cooler climes.

Slender Violet

Hybanthus monopetalus

This delicate, erect, herb-like shrub is common in sheltered spots in scrub and dry grassland in mountainous areas throughout much of eastern Australia and Tasmania. The leaves are narrow and soft, with the upper leaves held opposite, while the lower ones are mostly alternate. The striking blue flowers have five petals, but four of these are so tiny they are inconspicuous. The fifth is greatly elongated and its appearance gives rise to the botanical species name: *monopetalus* is Latin for single-petalled, and this feature gives the plant a highly distinctive appearance.

Identification: An erect, herb-like shrub, reaching 50cm/20in tall where ungrazed. The soft, narrow leaves are mid-green with a strongly defined midrib, 1–6cm/⅖–5¼in long. Large, solitary, prominent blue flowers are borne on slender stalks; they have five more or less equal sepals and five petals, four of which are inconspicuous. The fifth is 6–20mm/¼–¾in long, oval, pale blue with darker veins, with a pale spot toward the base and a broad, dilated concavity or claw in the base.

Distribution: Eastern Australia and Tasmania.
Height and spread: 50cm/20in.
Habit and form: Herb-like shrub.
Leaf shape: Linear-lanceolate.
Pollinated: Insect.

Above left: The fruit is divided into three parts that split to reveal the seed.

Left: While herb-like in appearance, slender violet is actually a shrub.

Australian Violet

Trailing violet, ivy violet, *Viola hederacea*

Known as the ivy violet because of its trailing habit, this creeping herbaceous plant is a native of shady and moist spots among the mountains of eastern and southern Australia, including Tasmania. It is a fairly variable species, with dark green leaves and, during the summer, short stems of fragrant, purple or white flowers that have a squashed appearance and are borne fairly abundantly above the foliage.

Identification: A stemless, tufted or creeping, mat-forming perennial. The leaves are rounded or kidney-shaped, up to 4cm/1½in wide, sometimes toothed, dark green with paler veination, often forming dense cover. The flowers are blue-violet to white, usually with a blue-purple centre and white edges, and are flattened in appearance, with bearded lateral petals and inconspicuous spurs. They are held 7.5cm/3in above the leaves and are sometimes scented.

Above: The flowers have a squashed appearance when they open.

Left: The flowerheads are pale and nodding before they open.

Distribution: Eastern and southern Australia.
Height and spread: 7.5cm/3in.
Habit and form: Mat-forming herb.
Leaf shape: Spathulate to reniform.
Pollinated: Insect.

Left: The flattened flowers are held on thin stalks above the foliage.

Red Passion Flower

Passiflora aurantia

This climbing vine is naturally found in eastern Queensland and also occurs in New Guinea and on some Pacific islands. *Passiflora* is a well-known genus because it includes the commercial passion fruit, *P. edulis*. While the genus is mostly restricted to areas of tropical America and Asia, this is one of three Australian species. It has tri-lobed leaves and red or salmon flowers, borne mainly in winter and spring, although a few can usually be seen all year round. The flowers deepen in colour as they age and are followed by egg-shaped, green fruits, which, although edible, are unpalatable.

Distribution: North-east Australia, New Guinea, Pacific islands.
Height and spread: Variable.
Habit and form: Liana.
Leaf shape: Lobed.
Pollinated: Insect.

Right: This vigorous climbing plant clings by means of coiling tendrils and flowers over a long period.

Identification: A vigorous, woody liana with hairless, angular stems, producing long, coiling tendrils by which it supports upward growth. The leaves, up to 7.5cm/3in long, usually have three shallow oval lobes. The flowers, up to 10cm/4in in diameter, have narrow, pale pink sepals deepening to orange-red, orange to brick-red petals and deep red filaments. The egg-shaped green fruit, 4cm/1½in long, contains greyish pulp and numerous black seeds.

OTHER PASSIONFLOWER, VIOLET AND SAXIFRAGE SPECIES OF NOTE

Mahoe Wao *Melicytus lanceolatus*
This large shrub or small tree from New Zealand has grey-brown bark and long, deep green leaves. The purple-tinged flowers are held in clusters of six around the leaf axils, although they sometimes appear to emerge directly from the branches. They are followed by small, dark purple fruits.

Whiteywood *Melicytus ramiflorus*
This is a fast-growing, spreading tree with a short, branched trunk and whitish-grey peeling bark. Found naturally all over New Zealand, Fiji, Norfolk Island and the Solomon Islands, it occurs from sea level to 900m/2950ft. The small yellow flowers are followed by blue or purple berries.

Mountain Violet *Viola cunninghamii*
This stemless, hairless perennial with rounded or triangular leaves is a native of New Zealand, where it is found in North, South, Stewart, and Chatham Islands, in moist or shady sites in river valleys. The short-spurred flowers appear in spring, and are white to pale violet, with greenish or yellowish throats and a number of purple lines on the petals.

Aupaka *Isodendrion hosakae*
This endemic Hawaiian shrub occurs on volcanic cinder or ash soils in the Waikoloa region. It is a branched, upright, evergreen with long, white, five-petalled, tubular flowers, which are produced from the axils of shiny leaves near the stem tips.

Wire Netting Bush

Corokia cotoneaster

This much-branched shrub with stiff interlacing branches is common throughout New Zealand, in dry rocky places from North Cape to Stewart Island. Its star-like yellow flowers are followed by red berries in autumn and, although the plant is an evergreen, the leaves are so small and scattered that even in full growth the plant has a sparse, metallic appearance. It is thought that the cage-like tangle of branches evolved to protect the tender young shoots from being eaten by the moa, New Zealand's giant bird, now extinct.

Distribution: New Zealand.
Height and spread: 2m/6½ft.
Habit and form: Shrub.
Leaf shape: Rounded.
Pollinated: Insect.

Identification: The slender, tortuous branches of this shrub are covered in silvery hairs, later becoming hairless, dark grey or black, often spiralling or tangled or zigzagging. The sparse, round leaves, up to 2cm/¾in across, are maroon-green or bronze, often flushed maroon above, silvery beneath. The solitary yellow flowers appear in the leaf axils or in a terminal panicle in late spring; they are star-like, with five narrow petals and five prominent stamens. The fruit is a small, vermilion, fleshy drupe with a persistent calyx.

Left: The stiff interlacing branches give rise to the common name of this shrub.

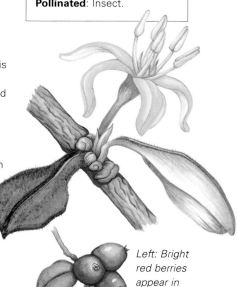

Left: Bright red berries appear in the autumn.

CARROT FAMILY

The Apiaceae, or carrot family, are poorly represented across much of Oceania although those that do occur there tend to be interesting examples, having become isolated from their counterparts in the Northern Hemisphere. A greater diversity of species is found in Australia and some of these have also evolved into interesting forms.

Sydney Flannel Flower

Actinotus helianthi

This herbaceous or shrubby plant, found in open forest and woodland and on dry hillsides, coastal dunes and heaths, usually on sand or sandstone, is a native of the coast and mountains of New South Wales and southern Queensland. The deeply lobed, grey leaves have a velvety texture, giving rise to the common name. The small flowers occur in clusters surrounded by velvety, petal-like bracts, giving each flowerhead an appearance similar to that of a daisy. The flowers appear in spring and continue into early summer, though some are usually present throughout the year.

Identification: An erect, branching, herbaceous or shrubby perennial. The pinnate leaves have narrow, toothed, felted segments and the daisy-like flowerheads consist of numerous tiny, white flowers in dense umbels surrounded by large cream bracts, often tipped green, with a dense covering of silvery, woolly hairs. They are followed by fluffy seeds in a globular head, readily dispersed by the breeze.

Distribution: Eastern Australia.
Height and spread: 60cm/2ft.
Habit and form: Herbaceous perennial or subshrub.
Leaf shape: Compound.
Pollinated: Insect.

Gingidia montana

This small, aromatic herbaceous plant is found in moist open sites in both the North and South Islands of New Zealand and is also endemic to New South Wales. It occurs in *Eucalyptus paucifolia* woodland, or more commonly at the edge of forests of southern beech, *Nothofagus* species, growing within the crevices of basalt or trachyte rocks, mostly on cliff faces.

Identification: A stout, hairless, erect herb or small shrub, up to 50cm/20in high, strongly aromatic with divided leaves up to 60cm (2ft) long, composed of seven to nine ovate to almost circular leaflets with obtusely toothed margins. The white flowers are borne on umbel-like inflorescences with 8–12 rays, up to 2.5cm/1in long, on 15cm/6in flowering stems. The fruits are egg-shaped. Plants occasionally hybridize with the related *Aciphilla squarrosa* and the exact details of its classification remain the subject of some debate.

Distribution: New Zealand and New South Wales.
Height and spread: 50cm/20in.
Habit and form: Herbaceous perennial or subshrub.
Leaf shape: Pinnate.
Pollinated: Insect.

Far left: Gingidia *forms dense masses of aromatic green foliage that resembles cress but is topped in summer by white umbels of flowers.*

Golden Speargrass

Bayonet plant, golden Spaniard, *Aciphylla aurea*

This common perennial, from the subalpine grasslands of New Zealand's South Island, forms a large, clumped rosette of stiff, rigid, yellowish-green leaves with golden-yellow margins, which can deliver a painful stab if not approached with care, hence the common name for this species. The spiny, golden flower spike that appears in summer is rather showy and contains many flowers. Individual plants are either male or female (dioecious) and this gives the species a slight variability. Its ability to survive fire has led to it colonizing extensive areas.

Identification: A coarse, evergreen perennial with rosettes up to 90cm/3ft across. The grey-green, spear-shaped leaves, up to 70cm/28in long, have thick sheaths and yellow margins and midribs. The flowers appear on a massive terminal panicle up to 90cm/3ft tall, usually long-stemmed and candelabra-like, composed of compound umbels. Those of the male plants are strictly unisexual, while the female flowers are interspersed with sporadic males. The small flowers are white to pale yellow and crowded, though the male umbels are more loosely arranged than the female's.

Distribution: South Island, New Zealand.
Height and spread: Evergreen herbaceous perennial.
Habit and form: Up to 90cm/3ft.
Leaf shape: Hastate.
Pollinated: Insect.

OTHER CARROT FAMILY SPECIES OF NOTE

Flannel Flower
Actinotus leucocephalus
This species from Western Australia has white, fuzzy or hairy bracts, making it look almost like an edelweiss when it flowers. Flowering is erratic, however: the best time to see flowers is in spring following a bushfire, when they sometimes cover the ground profusely.

Actinotus bellidioides
This rare species is restricted to peaty soils, chiefly in upland bogs in south-eastern Australia and Tasmania. It has a small, flat rosette of circular dark green leaves, which although not as hairy as other species are typical of the genus, and is identifiable chiefly by its buttercup-like, golden-yellow bracts.

Anisotome flexuosa
This large perennial has narrow, two-pinnate, leathery leaflets, and like others in the genus it is dioecious. It is found in montane and subalpine habitats of New Zealand's South Island, where it may be seen growing among rock crevices. The creamy-white umbels are loosely scattered across the hummocky mass of foliage in the early summer.

Aciphylla montana
This tufted, small perennial of South Island, New Zealand, has sharp-pointed, yellowish-green leaves, with two to four pairs of segments, which are strongly pungent when crushed. The male inflorescences are shorter than those of the female. The yellowish umbels rarely exceed the leaf height.

Aromatic Aniseed

Anisotome aromatica

This perennial herb, native to the South Island of New Zealand, is found chiefly in the grassland of the montane subalpine zones. The fragrant flowers are held in clusters in small umbels, which appear above the carpeting foliage. The male and female flowers appear on separate plants, both arranged in umbels on slender, sparingly divided stems.

Distribution: South Island, New Zealand.
Height and spread: 50cm/20in.
Habit and form: Herbaceous perennial.
Leaf shape: Pinnate.
Pollinated: Insect.

Identification: A dioecious herbaceous perennial with basal, pinnate leaves, 5–12cm/2–5in long, with 6–12 pairs of leathery, toothed, deeply divided leaflets, the segments of which are sessile and deeply divided with hairs at their apex. The flowers appear in clusters in a small umbel reaching 10–15cm/4–6in across and are white and fragrant. The male umbels are large and many flowered and the female umbels are much smaller, contracted and fewer flowered, often looking a little like a different species. Several sub-species occur across its range, making it a variable plant and one that can cause confusion when identifying it.

BELLFLOWER, PINCUSHION AND MADDER FAMILIES

Bellflowers (Campanulaceae) are highly ornamental and have become familiar plants in cultivation. The Australian family Brunoniaceae (pincushion family) has only one genus and species, whereas the Rubiaceae, the madder family, mostly occurs in the tropics.

Royal Bluebell

Wahlenbergia gloriosa

The royal bluebell occurs mainly in subalpine woodland above 1,300m/4,250ft in the Australian Capital Territory, south-eastern New South Wales and Victoria. It grows in the most uninviting dry, stony habitats, often exposed to full sun and strong winds. The vivid blue or violet-blue flowers are easily recognized; they are held above the foliage on long slender stems and may be erect or nodding. It has become scarce in recent times and is now legally protected throughout its natural range.

Identification: A small, slender, creeping to semi-erect herbaceous perennial with spreading rhizomes and erect stems, sometimes branching, rising above the oval, wavy-edged leaves. The flowers, 2.5cm/1in across, are deep blue to purple, bell-shaped, erect or nodding, on long slender stems with a few distant, narrow bracts; there are usually five petals, joined in a short tube, with spreading lobes with light blue bases and a purple style ending in two white stigmas. The fruit is a small capsule, prominently ribbed and surmounted by the five erect sepals.

Distribution: South-eastern Australia.
Height and spread: Variable.
Habit and form: Creeping herbaceous perennial.
Leaf shape: Obovate.
Pollinated: Insect.

Left: The small creeping stems of this herb give rise to vivid blue or violet-blue, star-shaped flowers.

Blue Pincushion

Brunonia australis

This silky or hairy herb is locally frequent in all Australian states in dry forests, being most often encountered following bushfires. Each inflorescence has a large number of crowded flowers, with the reproductive parts raised above the petals so that they resemble pins in a pincushion. The flowers appear in late spring to summer, held on leafless stems above the rosettes of silky, hairy, spoon-shaped leaves, giving the plant a decorative appearance. *Brunonia* is a monotypic genus although it is variable in habit as a result of its widespread distribution.

Identification: A rather variable, densely hairy herbaceous perennial, growing to 30cm/1ft tall and with grey-green, spoon-shaped leaves up to 5cm (2in) long, forming a basal rosette. The vivid cornflower-blue flowers, tubular at the base and with spreading, star-like petals, appear in crowded, terminal, pincushion-like heads up to 2.5cm/1in across, atop a base of hairy calyces and borne on erect, leafless stems that reach 45cm/18in tall, usually in spring but sporadically extending through to autumn.

Distribution: Australia.
Height and spread: 30cm/1ft.
Habit and form: Herbaceous perennial.
Leaf shape: Obovate.
Pollinated: Insect.

Beach Gardenia

Guettarda speciosa

Beach gardenia can be found in coastal northern Australia, from Western Australia to central Queensland, and also on many Pacific Islands, typically in beach strand communities in coastal regions, almost all the way to the high tide level in places. It has large rounded leaves, above which the large, white, fragrant, tubular flowers occur from spring to autumn, although they may also be seen at other times. The fragrance is similar to that of true gardenia, though weaker.

Distribution: North Australia, Pacific Islands.
Height and spread: 5m/16ft.
Habit and form: Shrub or small tree.
Leaf shape: Obovate.
Pollinated: Insect, probably moths.

Far right: Beach gardenia is a large, spreading shrub or small tree. It is very sensitive to too much sun and its flowers are most fragrant at night or just before dawn.

Identification: The leaves, up to 20cm/8in long, are opposite or in whorls of three, broadly oval with blunt or pointed tips, smooth above and hairy beneath, with a prominent midrib and 7–10 pairs of lateral nerves. White, fragrant, tubular flowers up to 4cm/1½in long, with seven spreading lobes, appear in dense axillary cymes, and are followed by small, hard, globular, white to brown fruits.

OTHER BELLFLOWER, PINCUSHION AND MADDER FAMILY SPECIES OF NOTE

Australian Bluebell *Wahlenbergia stricta*
This Australian flower is probably the most commonly encountered of the genus, being found everywhere except the Northern Territory and is often seen on roadsides. It forms clumps up to 40cm/16in high, and its masses of light blue or white flowers are easily seen, in spring and summer.

Indian Mulberry *Morinda citrifolia*
This large shrub to medium tree has oval leaves and white flowers that occur in the leaf axils in clusters, mainly in summer and autumn. These are followed by succulent fruits, which fuse into a large compound structure as they ripen. The fruits are edible but are very pungent when ripe, apparently to attract fruit bats.

Coprosma pumila
This small, mat-forming alpine shrub from Australia and New Zealand hugs the rocks among which it grows to form a tight cushion. The bases of the leaf stems are fused, giving a fleshy appearance. The lemon-yellow, star-shaped flowers are followed by yellow-red fleshy fruits.

Delissea rytidosperma
This unusual and rare flower is an Hawaiian endemic. Each tall upright stem is topped with a whorl of greyish-green, serrated leaves, sometimes tinged purple. The long, claw-shaped, pale green to purple flowers emerge from close to the growing point, in loose inflorescences.

Sweet Suzie

Canthium odoratum syn. *Psydrax odorata*

Sweet Suzie is a large shrub, with a range from Hawaii, Micronesia and parts of the South Pacific to the rainforest in northern Australia and more occasionally open forest on the continent. It is a common species in the Whitsunday area of north Queensland. It is a very handsome plant, with white bark that contrasts well with its dark, shiny leaves, but it is the clusters of attractive, sweetly fragrant flowers that arise from the leaf axils over a long season that earn this plant its common name.

Identification: A medium to large shrub, sometimes a small tree, with white bark and green young twigs. The oval leaves, up to 8cm/3¼in long, are glossy deep green on the top surface, duller below, with paler green veins and slightly wavy edges. The small, highly fragrant, tubular white flowers are borne in clusters arising from the leaf axils, appearing prolifically in spring and autumn. They are followed by fleshy, juicy, black fruits about 5mm/³⁄₁₆in in diameter, containing two seeds.

Distribution: Hawaii, Micronesia, South Pacific, northern Australia.
Height and spread: Variable.
Habit and form: Shrub or tree.
Leaf shape: Ovate.
Pollinated: Insect.

Below: Sweet Suzie grows into a small tree or large shrub.

NETTLE, DEADNETTLE AND VERBENA FAMILIES

The nettle family, Urticaceae, contains about 45 genera and 700 species, many of which have stinging hairs on their stems and leaves. The Lamiaceae, or deadnettle family, comprise 200 genera. Verbenaceae, the verbena family, has 75 genera and 3000 species, mostly tropical or subtropical herbs or trees.

Stinging Tree

Gympie-gympie, *Dendrocnide moroides*

This tropical member of the nettle family ranks as one of the most painful plant encounters should you ever be unlucky enough to touch it. In Australia it is officially classed as a dangerous plant. The stems and leaves are coated with fine hairs which, when embedded in the skin, cause severe pain and irritation. Apparently the plants have killed dogs and horses that have bumped into them. There is no effective antidote known for the stinging tree. These plants are mostly found along Australia's eastern coast, especially in the rain-forest of the north-east and, like other nettles, they tend to grow in disturbed areas, especially more open and sunny parts, such as forest clearings and riverbanks.

Identification: A single-stemmed herbaceous perennial or sparingly branched shrub, with stems up to 5cm/2in wide. The leaves are large and broad, oval or heart-shaped, up to 30cm/1ft long and 22cm/9in wide, on 5–15cm/2–6in leaf stalks. The small male and female flowers are borne on separate plants, in panicles in the forks of leaves.

Distribution: Queensland, Australia.
Height and spread: 90cm–5m/3–16ft.
Habit and form: Shrub.
Leaf shape: Ovate or cordate.
Pollinated: Wind.

Left: The single stem supports the large stinging leaves.

Far left: The fruits appear on female trees.

Victorian Christmas Bush

Victoria dogwood, mint bush, *Prostanthera lasianthos*

This spectacular summer-flowering tall shrub, or small tree, has white or pink flowers and is commonly seen growing along the banks of streams or gullies in south-east Australia and Tasmania. It flowers profusely around December, hence the common name. It emits a strong scent similar to eucalyptus or peppermint when brushed. In favourable conditions the Christmas bush flowers so heavily that the fallen flowers form a carpet on the ground beneath.

Identification: A variable woody species with long, smooth, upright shoots and lance-shaped, soft, slightly fleshy, opposite leaves 5–7.5cm/2–3in long with toothed edges, paler below. The fragrant flowers, appearing in summer, are paired in short leafless racemes, forming branched terminal panicles up to 15cm/6in long. The flowers are funnel-shaped with five lobes, two forming the upper lip and three the spreading lower lip. They are white or cream, or may be tinted violet or lilac, spotted brown or yellow in the wide throat and covered inside and out with fine hairs.

Distribution: Eastern Australia.
Height and spread: 8m/26ft.
Habit and form: Tall shrub or small tree.
Leaf shape: Lanceolate.
Pollinated: Insect.

Right: The Christmas bush can be a shrub or small tree.

Above and right: The white flowers are peppermint-scented.

Honohono

Haplostachys haplostachya

Distribution: Hawaii.
Height and spread:
30–60cm/1–2ft.
Habit and form: Subshrub.
Leaf shape: Variable/ovate.
Pollinated: Insect.

This extremely rare plant, formerly from Kauai, Maui and Hawaii, is now known only from a single population in Kipukakalawamauna on Hawaii. The genus is endemic to the islands and comprises five species, all extinct except for a few remaining plants of this species. It is found on dry shrublands and forests on old lava flows and cinder cones. Though a member of the mint family, it lacks the characteristic aromatic oils, probably because they had no natural pests on the island. The woolly leaves help to reflect sunlight away from the plant, and the beautiful spikes of sweet-smelling, white flowers appear at the branch tips.

Left: The plant forms an erect hairy sub-shrub.

Right: The flowerhead.

Identification: Erect, herbaceous perennial or subshrub with four-angled stems. The opposite, lance-shaped or oval to triangular leaves are extremely soft, covered with dense, tangled or matted woolly hairs, light green on top and silvery-white underneath. The irregular, funnel-shaped flowers are large, white and fragrant, up to 5cm/2in long, borne on terminal racemes up to 45cm/18in tall, each bearing several flowers, arranged spirally around the stem. Four black, hard nutlets are produced per flower.

Left: The striking, white, fragrant flowers appear at the branch tips.

OTHER NETTLE, DEADNETTLE AND VERBENA FAMILY SPECIES OF NOTE

Snakebush *Hemiandra pungens*
This native of the coastal sands and woodlands of south-western Australia is a small shrub, sometimes prostrate or trailing. Tubular mauve to red flowers, with a two-lobed upper lip and a three-lobed lower lip, open in spring.

Austral Bugle *Ajuga australis*
This widespread native of Southern and Eastern Australia can be found in a range of soils and habitats. It is a small, herbaceous perennial with a basal rosette of velvety leaves and soft, erect stems. The flowers, usually deep blue or purple are seen mainly in spring and summer.

Lambstails *Lachnostachys verbascifolia*
Native to the deserts of Western Australia, lambstails is recognizable by its fluffy texture and white to grey colouring. Found in sandy places, especially the sand plains, its hairy covering protects it from the heat, although this almost entirely hides the tiny, pinkish flowers.

Mintplant *Chloanthes parviflora*
A small, erect, shrubby perennial, superficially resembling rosemary and found in Queensland and New South Wales, Australia. It reaches 60cm/2ft tall, and the pale mauve, hairy, tubular flowers are borne close to the axils of the stems through winter and spring.

Snowy Oxera

Royal creeper, *Oxera pulchella*

This evergreen, woody vine, like the rest of the genus, is found only in the dense, moist tropical forests of the Pacific island of New Caledonia. It has thick, deep green, rounded leaves on twining stems, which in turn sport large clusters of white, azalea-shaped, pendent bells with a hint of cream-yellow. It tends to scramble over smaller bushes, rather than climb taller trees.

Identification: A climbing, evergreen, twining shrub, with rough bark and prominent lenticels, and smooth stems to 5cm/2in thick. The leathery, dark green, oblong to lance-shaped leaves, opposite and up to 12.5cm/5in long, have smooth or toothed margins. The flowers appear in great abundance in axillary, forked cymes, in early spring; 5cm/2in or more long, they are pendent, brilliant white or yellow-white.

Distribution: New Caledonia.
Height and spread: Variable.
Habit and form: Vining shrub.
Leaf shape: Oblong.
Pollinated: Insect.

Above: The buds are conspicuous.

Left: Oxera forms a climbing evergreen vine.

FIGWORT AND MYOPORUM FAMILIES

The Scrophulariaceae (figwort family) comprise mostly herbs but also a few small shrubs, with about 190 genera and 4,000 predominately temperate species, with a cosmopolitan distribution. The majority are found in temperate areas and tropical mountains. The Myoporaceae (myoporum family) comprise four genera and 150 species, mostly trees and shrubs, and found in Australia and the South Pacific.

Spotted Emu Bush

Eremophila maculata

This shrub is one of the most widespread and variable of the emu bushes, a large genus of 214 species, all endemic to Australia. It can be found in inland areas of all mainland states, mostly on clay soils in the more arid regions. It is a variable plant with tubular, nectar-filled flowers, which occur in the leaf axils and are seen in a wide range of colours from pink and mauve to red, orange and yellow. They often have a pale, spotted throat. Flowering occurs mainly through winter and spring but some flowers may also be seen at other times.

Identification: An evergreen shrub with downy twigs and alternate, narrow leaves. Abundant tubular flowers in a wide range of colours are borne in the axils: they are about 2.5cm/1in long, constricted at the base, with protruding stamens and spotted, hairy throats; the upper lip consists of four erect lobes, the lower lip is reflexed and deeply divided. The fruit is a drupe with four chambers, each containing one or more seeds, subtended by the persistent five-lobed calyx.

Distribution: Australia.
Height and spread: l–2.5m/3–8ft.
Habit and form: Shrub.
Leaf shape: Linear.
Pollinated: Insect.

Left: The emu bush is variable in habit, and often forms a small tree-like bush.

Slender Myoporum

Myoporum floribundum

This spectacular but uncommon myoporum occurs naturally on the coastal ranges of southern New South Wales and Victoria, Australia, rising up to gullies of the upper Snowy River and parts of the Southern Tablelands. It is a slender, fragrant shrub, and has long, arching branches with pendulous, narrow, sticky leaves and small, scented, white flowers that cluster along the branches on fine hair-like stalks, giving a feathery appearance to the massed inflorescences in spring and early summer.

Identification: A spindly shrub with an arching or weeping habit. The very narrow leaves, up to 9cm/3½in long, alternate, are smooth and dark green, and hang down from the horizontal or arching branches, giving the plant a wilted look. Small, scented, white to cream, five-petalled flowers, with prominent stamens, are borne on fine stalks in the axil of each leaf, and are clustered along the upper parts of the branches, which often arch under the weight. The fruits are numerous, small, succulent and brown when mature.

Distribution: South-eastern Australia.
Height and spread: 2.5m/8ft.
Habit and form: Shrub.
Leaf shape: Narrow.
Pollinated: Insect.

Left: The long arching branches form a slender, weeping shrub in time.

Snowy Mountain Foxglove

Ourisia macrocarpa

Distribution: New Zealand.
Height and spread: Up to 60cm/2ft.
Habit and form: Alpine herb.
Leaf shape: Rounded.
Pollinated: Insect, probably flies.

This New Zealand alpine flower is found chiefly in the southern mountains of the South Island and is a low-growing, rhizomatous perennial that flowers during spring or early summer according to location. It spreads to form a loose mat of dark leathery leaves from which the whorled inflorescences emerge on long stalks. Like many alpine species in New Zealand, the flowers are white and relatively unspecialized, reflecting the limited range of native insects available to pollinate them.

Identification: A low-growing, alpine perennial herb with robust, erect stems up to 60cm/2ft long, though usually shorter, rising from a creeping rhizome. The oval to circular leaves are thick and leathery, dark green above, hairless except on the margins, which have rounded teeth. The tubular, white flowers appear in sequentially blooming whorls on the stout stems; they are up to 2.5cm/1in in diameter, with a broad, short tube and five spreading lobes, sometimes with a yellow throat, minutely hairy within.

OTHER FIGWORT AND MYOPORUM FAMILY SPECIES OF NOTE

New Zealand Mousehole Tree
Myoporum laetum
A small tree with alternate, glossy green, finely toothed leaves, covered with translucent glands that give them an attractive appearance. The flowers appear in summer from the leaf axils and are white spotted with purple; while attractive, they are easily overlooked. The fruits that follow are oblong and reddish.

Ourisia integrifolia
This small herb of alpine wet areas appears to be closely related to the New Zealand *Ourisia* species and is the only representative of the genus in Australia. It is restricted to Tasmania, where it can be found in thickets and woods. The shiny leaves are very small in comparison to the large white or pale blue, five-petalled flowers, which appear in summer.

Parahebe lyallii
This variable plant can be found in many parts of New Zealand. The flowers are most commonly white or white with pink, held over the reddish-green leaves in spring. As its name suggests, the genus is closely allied to hebes, but in appearance it resembles a small, slightly shrubby *Veronica* species.

Hebe elliptica
This bushy shrub has fleshy, green, oval leaves with light edges. The flowers, which open in the spring, are white to pale mauve and relatively large. It has a variable habit, and is found on the west coasts of the South and North Islands of New Zealand and also in the Falkland Islands.

New Zealand Hebe

Hebe speciosa

This bushy, rounded shrub is highly popular with gardeners, but in the wild is found only in a few localities in the Marlborough Sounds and on the west coast of North Island on exposed sea cliffs. It is a highly variable species, giving rise to many cultivars and hybrids, some of which may have become naturalized outside its native range. Its large, magenta inflorescences make it one of the more spectacular hebes when flowering commences in summer and extends over a long season.

Identification: A strong-growing shrub with stout, angular branches and thick fleshy, glossy, leaves up to l0cm/4in long. The stems and margins of the young leaves are purple, and this colour persists on the backs of the leaves when they mature. The flowers are dark red to magenta, crowded in terminal conical to cylindrical racemes up to 7cm/2¾in long.

Distribution: North Island, New Zealand.
Height and spread: 2m/6½ft.
Habit and form: Shrub.
Leaf shape: Ovate.
Pollinated: Insect.

Left: Hebe forms a small- to medium-sized rounded bush that is often found in cultivation.

AGAVE, GRASS TREE, BLOODWORT AND LILY FAMILIES

The agave (Agavaceae), grass tree (Xanthorrhoeaceae), and bloodwort families (Haemodoraceae) are all loosely allied to the lily family (Liliaceae). They generally prefer hot dry habitats and are well represented in Australia and New Zealand.

New Zealand Cabbage Tree

Cabbage palm, *Cordyline australis*

This unusual-looking tree typically occurs on forest margins and coastal cliffs, in swamps and other wet areas, and is a familiar sight throughout New Zealand. It is also widely planted in gardens and is known to many who have never visited its native islands. The species is often naturalized outside its range and there are many cultivars. The crown is made up of long, bare branches carrying bushy heads of large, grass-like leaves, from which large panicles of small, white, sweet-scented flowers emerge. Flowering is erratic, with the best displays usually following dry summers.

Identification: The trunk is generally sparingly or not at all branched below, copiously branched above, and ultimately massive, up to 1.5m/5ft in diameter, with rough, fissured bark. The leaves 30–90cm/1–3ft long and 5cm/2in wide, are narrow and arching, light green with indistinct veins. Small, sweetly fragrant flowers, creamy-white with yellow anthers, appear in a much-branched panicle up to 1.8m/6ft long and 60cm/2ft wide, with well-spaced branches more or less at right angles and almost hidden by the flowers. The small, spherical fruits are white or very pale blue.

Distribution: New Zealand.
Height and spread: Up to 20m/65ft x 4m/13ft.
Habit and form: Tree.
Leaf shape: Linear-lanceolate.
Pollinated: Insect.

Left: The small flowers are fragrant and held in dense panicles.

Right: The palm-like trunks are distinctive.

New Zealand Flax

Phormium tenax

This robust, evergreen, New Zealand perennial gets its common name because the Maori people used the leaf fibres for making clothing, fishing nets and ropes. It is abundant, especially in lowland swamps and intermittently flooded land, and is also found on Norfolk Island. It has attractive foliage and, while not renowned for its flowers, the tubular, orange-red flowers that appear in tall, upright panicles are very striking.

Identification: A perennial rhizomatous herb with short, stout stems and strap-like, deep green leaves that are bright orange towards the base. They are stiff and erect, at least in the lower part, 90cm–3m/3–10ft long and 5–12.5cm/2–5in wide, usually splitting at the tip, clump-forming and fibrous. The smooth, dark brown flowering stems may reach a height of 5m/16ft. The flowers have dull red tepals, 2.5–5cm/1–2in long, with slightly recurved, orange tips to the inner tepals. The fruit is a long, three-sided capsule.

Distribution: New Zealand, Norfolk Island.
Height and spread: 2m/6½ft.
Habit and form: Rhizomatous herb.
Leaf shape: Linear-lanceolate.
Pollinated: Insect.

Left: The orange-red flowers appear in large panicles on long stems.

Tall Kangaroo Paw

Evergreen kangaroo paw, *Anigozanthos flavidus*

Distribution: South-west Australia.
Height and spread: 90cm/3ft.
Habit and form: Clump-forming perennial.
Leaf shape: Linear-lanceolate.
Pollinated: Insect.

This unusual plant, which is native to moist areas in open forests of the far south-west of Australia, has a vigorous clumping growth habit with long, dull green leaves. The tall flowering stems, which emerge from the bases of the leaves from late spring to midsummer, carry unusual furry flowers, which are mostly green, although they can also contain yellow or soft red tones. It is very attractive to birds, the prime pollinators.

Identification: A robust perennial with narrow olive to mid-green leaves 30–45cm/12–18in long and up to 4cm/1¾in wide. The reddish flowering stems are 90cm–3m/3–10ft long, smooth at the base becoming downy on the branches; the flowers, borne in panicles, have forward-pointing lobes that are usually sulphur-yellow to lime-green, though sometimes red, orange, pink or multi-coloured, and are densely covered with yellow-green or red-brown hairs.

Above: The unusual green, furry flowerheads emerge from the base of the stems.

OTHER AGAVE, GRASS TREE AND BLOODWORT SPECIES OF NOTE

Narrow-leaved Palm Lily *Cordyline stricta*
This shrubby, palm-like plant is found in wet forest and rainforest in Australia. It forms a multi-caned, fountain-shaped bush 2–3m/ 6½–10ft tall, with narrow, purplish dark green leaves. The showy, lavender to bluish flowers, in drooping panicles, appear in the spring and are followed by round, blue-black, fleshy fruits.

Mountain Flax *Phormium colensoi*
The mountain flax, while similar to *P. tenax*, is smaller, with thinner leaves that are arching rather than erect. The flowers are greenish-yellow and the seedpods are twisted and hang down from the flowering stalks.

Grass Tree *Xanthorrhoea australis*

This very slow-growing plant develops a rough trunk with age, coloured black as the result of surviving many bushfires. The long, narrow leaves are crowded at the tops of the trunks, and small, individual, white or cream flowers are clustered together in a spear-like spike, which can tower 2m/6½ft or more above the top of the trunk.

Western Australian Grass Tree *Kingia australis*
This unusual species is not related to true grasses. The sole species in this genus is found between Perth and Albany. It flowers irregularly, usually after a fire, with yellow, green and brown flowers appearing in early spring, amid the mass of grass-like leaves.

Blue Tinsel Lily

Calectasia cyanea

This plant takes its name from its shiny blue flowers, which really do have the look and feel of tinsel and appear mainly in late spring. Native to Western and South Australia, the bush is adapted to very dry conditions and resembles a small paperbark or tea tree, *Melaleuca* species, when not in flower. Despite its appearance, however, this monotypic genus is actually most closely related to the grass trees, *Xanthorrhoea* species.

Identification: A small rhizomatous shrub with upright slender stems clothed with small, needle-like sheathed leaves, spirally arranged. The solitary, bright blue flowers are borne terminally on short branchlets. They are star-like, with six pointed, glossy, metallic tepals and yellow anthers that turn red as they mature. The fruit is a one-seeded nut.

Below: The shiny, blue, star-like flowers give rise to this plant's common name.

Distribution: Southern Australia.
Height and spread: 25cm/10in.
Habit and form: Shrub.
Leaf shape: Linear-lanceolate.
Pollinated: Insect.

DAISY FAMILY

Australia and New Zealand support many species in the Asteraceae, or daisy family, many of which form impressive displays in summer or following rains in arid areas. It is on some of the islands in the vast southern oceans where plants have become isolated from their continental ancestors that the most interesting forms are encountered though.

Bachelor's Buttons

Billy buttons, *Craspedia uniflora*

This rosette-forming annual or sometimes perennial plant is found over a wide range of habitats in southern Australia, Tasmania and New Zealand, preferring dry, stony grassland, from lowland to moderate altitudes. The round pompom flowerheads that appear in the summer give rise to its common name; they are yellow in this species, although most other species in the genus have white flowers.

Above and left: The plant forms a low rosette of leaves.

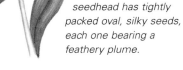

Above: The seedhead has tightly packed oval, silky seeds, each one bearing a feathery plume.

Identification: The erect flowering stems rise above basal rosettes of oval to narrowly spoon-shaped leaves up to 12.5cm/5in long. The yellow flowerheads are spherical, about 15mm/⅝in across, on very thin stems.

Distribution: Southern Australia, Tasmania and New Zealand.
Height and spread: 40cm/16in.
Habit and form: Rosette-forming annual.
Leaf shape: Oblong-ovate to spathulate.
Pollinated: Insect.

Swan River Daisy

Brachycome iberidifolia

This wiry annual plant has dainty, dark-eyed, bright blue, daisy-like, fragrant flowers, borne above and among the feathery leaves. It flowers predominantly in the cooler wetter months of the year. The plant is bushy or spreading in habit, and has downy, grey-green leaves that are deeply lobed.

Identification: An annual herb with slender, branched, glandular-hairy stems and finely divided, fern-like leaves up to 10cm/4in long. The daisy-like flowers, on slender stalks about 7.5cm/3in long, are white, blue or violet with yellow central discs. The fruit is tiny and club shaped with tiny bristles on the uppermost part.

Distribution: South and Western Australia.
Height and spread: 45cm/18in.
Habit and form: Annual herb.
Leaf shape: Pinnatifid.
Pollinated: Insect.

Below: The plant forms a low, spreading, wiry mass of feathery-leaved stems.

Left: A massed flowering of this plant is a spectacular sight.

Above: Pink flowerheads are rare or absent from wild populations but often selected in cultivated stock.

Winged Everlasting

Sandflower, *Ammobium alatum*

A native of sandy habitats in New South Wales and as far north as Queensland, Australia, the common name of this grey-leaved, perennial herb refers in part to the curious, membranous wings on its stems. In addition, the small flowerheads are surrounded by rows of papery bracts, giving the spent flowers an "everlasting" effect. The flowers are often dried for commercial use, being cut for drying just as they open.

Distribution:
Eastern Australia.
Height and spread:
50–90cm/20–36in.
Habit and form: Erect perennial.
Leaf shape: Lanceolate.
Pollinated: Insect.

Above: The papery bracts are tightly folded and enclose the yellow flowerhead in the bud.

Left: This grey-leaved herb has tall flower stems that emerge from a basal rosette.

Identification: The stems of this erect, branched perennial herb have wings formed from decurrent leaf bases. The pointed leaves, up to 18cm/7in long in the basal rosette, becoming smaller up the stem, are covered in white down. The flowerheads, with silvery-white, pointed, papery bracts and yellow centres, are about 2cm/¾in in diameter, borne singly at the ends of the flower stalks.

OTHER DAISY FAMILY SPECIES OF NOTE

Strawflower *Helichrysum bracteatum*
Also known as the yellow paper daisy, this coarse, erect perennial is relatively common across much of Australia, growing in open scrub and grassland areas. It gets its name from the papery texture of the bright yellow flowers, which close in the evening or on overcast days.

Celmisia hookeri
This large, tufted plant inhabits mountain grassland scrub and is confined to north-east Otago on the South Island of New Zealand. The broad green leaves are dark and leathery and large, white daisy flowers with yellow centres appear in the spring and summer.

Wilkesia gymnoxiphium
Endemic to Kauai in the Hawaiian Islands on dry volcanic soils, with rosettes elevated on woody stems up to 5m/16ft tall, the plant flowers once in its variable lifespan and then dies. The tall flower spike is composed of many nodding yellow flowers.

Mountain Daisy *Celmisia angustifolia*
This small subshrub, woody at its base, is found in the montane tussock grasslands of New Zealand. Its branches are clothed in old leaf remains. It has long, spoon-shaped leaves, with felted undersides, in rosettes at the branch tips. The white flowerheads are produced on solitary stalks during the summer.

Hawaiian Silversword

Ahinahina, *Argyroxiphium sandwicense*

This rosette-forming shrub is restricted to habitats in the cinders of volcanoes, at altitudes of up to 3,700m/12,000ft on the islands of Hawaii and Maui. It is a spectacular species, with tall maroon flowers surmounting the rounded rosette of silvery, sword-like leaves and making it one of the wonders of the Pacific plant world. The flowers develop erratically, usually between early summer and autumn. The grey hairy leaves are an indication of the harshness of the dry environment that this plant occupies.

Identification: A rosette-forming shrub that is usually solitary, with a short vegetative stem and a flowering stem up to 2.5m/8ft tall and 90cm/3ft wide. The pointed leaves, up to 40cm/16in long, are rigid, succulent, and covered with silvery hairs. They are spirally arranged, together forming a silver sphere. The showy inflorescence may contain between 50 and 600 compound flowerheads, pink or red in colour with yellow central disc florets.

Distribution: Hawaii and Maui.
Height and spread: 3m x 90cm/10 x 3ft.
Habit and form: Rosette-forming shrub.
Leaf shape: Lanceolate.
Pollinated: Probably insect.

Below: The tall showy inflorescence appears erratically between summer and autumn.

HEATH FAMILY

The Ericaceae, or heath family, are a large family, mostly shrubby in character, comprising about 125 genera and 3,500 species. Mostly lime-hating and restricted to acid soils, the family is cosmopolitan in distribution, except in deserts. It is almost absent from Australasia, where it is largely replaced by Epacridaceae, a family almost exclusively centred upon the Australian continent and nearby islands.

Giant Grass Tree

Tree heath, pandani, *Richea pandanifolia*

The wet mountain forests of Tasmania are home to this unusual plant, one of about ten species in the genus, all but one of which are endemic to the island. It is a tall, palm-like species, which usually grows on a single stem but may occasionally be branched. Its tapering leaves, with bases that wrap completely around the stem, are densely crowded towards the top of the trunk. The white or deep pink flower panicles arise from the leaf axils, often hidden among the leaves.

Identification: A gaunt evergreen tree or shrub with erect, slender branches with annual scars. The narrow, arching leaves, up to 90cm/3ft long, are crowded at the branch tips. They are smooth and waxy, with a concave upper surface and smooth or serrated margins tapering to a fine point, ultimately very slender and frayed. The white or pink flowers are inconspicuous, in erect axillary panicles crowded at the branch tips. The individual flowers are covered by large bracts, which fall as the flowers develop. The fruit is a capsule.

Distribution: Tasmania.
Height and spread: 10m/33ft.
Habit and form: Tree or shrub.
Leaf shape: Lanceolate.
Pollinated: Insect or bird.

Left: The flower panicles often go unnoticed as they are hidden among the leaves.

Pink Heath

Common heath, *Epacris impressa*

Found throughout the heaths and open forests of southern New South Wales, Victoria, Tasmania and eastern South Australia, the deep pink-flowered form of *E. impressa* is the floral emblem of Victoria. Usually a small shrub, its stiff branches have small leaves with a sharp point at the end and the narrow, tubular flowers occur in clusters along their tips. They contain copious nectar and are frequented by honey-eating birds. Their colour ranges from white through various shades of pink to bright red. Flowering occurs from autumn through to spring, reaching a peak in winter. A form from the Grampian Ranges in western Victoria known as *E. impressa* var. *grandiflora*, has larger flowers and leaves than the typical form and some plants have double flowers.

Identification: An often spindly, upright shrub, with stiff branches, russet when old, with stringy bark. The small, alternate leaves are narrow and sharply pointed. The flowers are snow-white to rose-pink or purple-red, short-stalked and nodding, borne in clusters in an elongated, slender, erect terminal raceme; the corolla tube, up to 2cm/¾in long, has five small indentations near the base, alternating with the stamens.

Distribution: South-east Australia.
Height and spread: 90cm/3ft.
Habit and form: Shrub.
Leaf shape: Linear-lanceolate.
Pollinated: Bird.

Left: The small pointed branches of this plant give it a rather spindly appearance.

Red Five Corners

Styphelia tubiflora

Distribution: Australia (except Northern Territory).
Height and spread: 1.5m/5ft.
Habit and form: Shrub.
Leaf shape: Oblong-linear.
Pollinated: Insect or bird.

Far right: The bright red flowers appear toward the branch tips in groups of twos or threes.

This genus, closely related to *Epacris*, contains 14 species, all of which occur naturally only in Australia and in all states except the Northern Territory. The fruit, a greenish-red berry with distinct ribs, gives rise to the common name. This species is found in dry forest or heath on the coast and mountains and has bright red flowers, emerging from greenish-yellow bases in autumn and spring.

Identification: A small straggly plant with stiff stems and small, narrow leaves with margins curved under, ending in a sharp point. The flowers, which appear from autumn to spring, are solitary or in loose groups of two or three, borne along the upper reaches of the branches in an apparent raceme; they are usually bright red, although white, pink and yellow forms are sometimes seen, with a greenish-yellow calyx. The corolla tube is narrow and about 2.5cm/1in long, conspicuously five-angled, with short lobes strongly rolled back to expose the long, protruding stamens. The fruit is a ribbed drupe with up to five seeds.

OTHER HEATH FAMILY SPECIES
OF NOTE

Blunt-leaf Heath *Epacris obtusifolia*
This uncommon small Australian shrub is found in sandy heathland along the coast from Queensland to Tasmania and has very small leaves, pressed to the stem. The large, bell-shaped white flowers appear in late winter and spring, in a massed display along the branches from the leaf axils, and are frequented by honey-eating birds.

Coral Heath *Epacris microphylla*
This shrub has tiny, pointed leaves, held erect against the wiry stems and angular branches. Common on damp rocky heath on the eastern coast of Australia, it is spectacular when in flower with masses of white, cup-shaped blooms toward the ends of the branches.

Richea dracophylla
This erect, small, evergreen shrub from Tasmania has sharp, pointed leaves arranged in a crowded spiral at the end of the stem. The dense spikes of white flowers appear at the ends of branches in autumn. When the flowers open the petals fall, giving the spike a bristly appearance.

Snow Bush *Leucopogon melaleucoides*
This very small shrub from east coast Australia is covered in tiny, hairy, tubular, white flowers, with pinkish calyces and a musty scent. The flowers appear in late winter to early spring. The plant resembles a small *Melaleuca* when not in flower.

Kerosene Bush

Richea scoparia

The kerosene bush provides brilliant splashes of colour throughout the alpine areas of Tasmania during the summer. While endemic to this island, it is a very common alpine and subalpine shrub of high rainfall areas. Its sharp leaves are persistent for a long time on old growth, making it unpopular with bushwalkers because it forms dense, prickly thickets. In summer, the terminal spikes of red, pink, white or orange flowers attract small lizards that feed on the nectar, and expose the plants reproductive organs to pollinating insects.

Identification: A bushy, erect, evergreen treelet or shrub. The semi-rigid, sharp-pointed, glossy leaves are up to 5cm/2in long, alternate, parallel-veined, on a sheathing stem with overlapping bases, persisting for several seasons. The flowers grow in dense, cylindrical terminal racemes up to 30cm/1ft long, and may be white, pink or orange. The corolla, up to 1.5cm/⅝in long, is closed at the tip except for a small opening, not separated into lobes.

Right: This prickly bush is often covered in brilliantly coloured flowers in the summer months.

Distribution: Tasmania.
Height and spread: 150 x 90cm/5 x 3ft.
Habit and form: Tree or shrub.
Leaf shape: Lanceolate.
Pollinated: Insect.

MALLOW AND ELAEOCARPUS FAMILIES

The Malvaceae, or mallow family, are not particularly well represented in Australia and Oceania, but those that do grow there include some strikingly beautiful flowers and some very rare plants among their numbers. The Elaeocarpaceae, or elaeocarpus family, are sparsely represented in Australia, mostly restricted to the eastern coast, but better represented on New Zealand.

Blue Hibiscus

Lilac hibiscus, *Alyogyne huegelii* syn. *Hibiscus huegelii*

The blue hibiscus is native to sandy and sandy-gravel soils in south and western Australia. Despite its common name, it is only distantly related to the true *Hibiscus*, and the flower colour ranges from pink or lilac to purple, usually with a contrasting basal spot. White and yellow forms also occur with the white form reported to have a more sprawling growth habit and brighter green leaves. Numerous varieties exist. The hibiscus-like flowers are borne singly in the leaf axils, appearing from spring through summer to autumn, and although individual flowers are short-blooming, only lasting a day or two; new flowers continue to open over a long period, generally in summer and autumn.

Identification: A fast-growing, medium-sized shrub with bright green, wrinkled, complexly five-lobed leaves and woolly younger stems. The conspicuous, short-lived but profusely borne flowers are about 7.5cm/3in across, with spreading, triangular to round, spirally overlapping petals and a staminal column with numerous filaments in whorls. They are usually lilac with reddish-purple-spotted throats, but may also be pink, blue, white or yellow.

Distribution: South and Western Australia.
Height and spread: 2.5m/8ft.
Habit and form: Shrub.
Leaf shape: Ovate-palmate lobed.
Pollinated: Insect.

Lily of the Valley Tree

Blueberry ash, *Elaeocarpus reticulatus*

Elaeocarpus is a genus of about 200 species occurring in eastern Australia and in nearby tropical areas, but the blueberry ash is unique among these in extending south into temperate areas. It can be found as far south as Flinders Island and Tasmania, where it grows in forest gullies and wooded ranges, usually near the coast. Flowering occurs in summer, when masses of small, bell-shaped flowers with an unusual, liquorice scent are produced. The flowers are followed by globular, blue fruits, which are retained on the plant for a long time, attracting many bird species.

Identification: A small tree with a dense crown of foliage and an approximately conical form. The branchlets and leaf stalks are often reddish, with distinct leaf scars. The leaves are alternate, 10–15cm/4–6in long, oval or lance-shaped with pointed tips, dark green above with prominent veins, paler below. Lax axillary racemes appear from mid-spring to midsummer; the fragrant flowers are small, cup-shaped, ivory-white, with three to five fringed petals and numerous stamens. The fruit is a tough, blue, globular drupe, about 12mm/½in in diameter, with a thin layer of edible flesh and one seed encased in a hard, rough stone.

Distribution: Eastern Australia.
Height and spread: 3–15 x 5m/10–50 x 16ft.
Habit and form: Tree.
Leaf shape: Oblong-elliptic.
Pollinated: Bird.

Far left: The globular fruits are popular with birds.

Left: This small tree has a dense crown.

Mountain Ribbonwood

Lacebark, *Hoheria lyallii*

This large shrub or small tree is found by forest edges and streams in the drier, eastern, reaches of the Southern Alps of New Zealand, at altitudes between 600–1,050m/2,000–3,500ft, where it forms scrub-like groves on the upper margins of the forests. Large quantities of flowers are borne in the leaf axils in summer or autumn, when they can be so profuse as to bend the flexible branches.

Distribution: South Island, New Zealand.
Height and spread: 6m/20ft.
Habit and form: Tree.
Leaf shape: Cordate.
Pollinated: Insect.

Right: Mountain ribbonwood is mostly restricted to high water-courses and damp forest margins.

Far right: Ribbonwood forms a large shrub or small tree that flowers profusely in late summer.

Identification: A deciduous tree with alternate, heart-shaped, grey-green, deeply toothed leaves 5–10cm/2–4in long and up to 5cm/2in wide. Mature leaves are covered in white down, especially on the undersides, while the juvenile foliage is smooth. The five-petalled, snow-white flowers are 2.5cm/1in in diameter, on slender stalks with densely hairy calyces, yellow filaments and purple anthers. The round fruit breaks up into 10–15, compressed, downy, slightly winged carpels.

OTHER MALLOW AND ELAEOCARPUS FAMILY SPECIES OF NOTE

New Zealand Damson *Elaeocarpus dentatus*
This tall forest tree with grey bark is found in lowland forests on both the North and South Islands. The leaves are quite tough and leathery, and have wavy to serrated margins. Clusters of white, bell-shaped flowers appear in summer, followed by purple drupes in the autumn.

Sturt's Desert Rose *Gossypium sturtianum*
This wild cotton species is widely distributed in the interior of Australia and is the floral emblem of the Northern Territory. It is a shrub with large oval leaves and showy, hibiscus-like, pink to mauve flowers with a dark red centre. The flowers can be seen for most of the year, with a peak in late winter.

Native Rosella
Abelmoschus moschatus subsp. *tuberosus*
Found in northern Australia, this plant dies back to an underground tuber in the dry season, emerging again following the first substantial rains. The dark-centred, pink-white or cream, hibiscus-like blooms, last for one day only but are prolific between October and April.

Hawaiian White Hibiscus *Hibiscus waimeae*
This rare Hawaiian endemic species, found only on Kauai, occurs in two distinct and isolated populations on opposite sides of the island. The single white flowers last only one day, opening in the morning and fading to pink in the afternoon.

Phillip Island Hibiscus

Hibiscus insularis

This island endemic is confined to just two patches on Phillip Island. Remarkably, these have survived despite the grazing pigs, goats and rabbits, which destroyed most of the island's other vegetation, although the removal of these introduced animals is allowing new seedlings to regenerate near the original bushes. The plant is very attractive and produces creamy flowers, which fade to a beautiful wine colour for about 10 months of the year. It has tiny, neat leaves and a densely branching characteristic, that are adaptations to the strong coastal winds of its native habitat and this has made it popular with gardeners in recent years.

Distribution: Phillip Island.
Height and spread: 3.5m/12ft.
Habit and form: Evergreen shrub.
Leaf shape: Ovate when young more cordate with age.
Pollinated: Insect.

Identification: A dense, bushy, many-branched shrub, growing up to 3.5m/12ft in tall, with a spread of 1.8m/6ft. There is a marked difference between the juvenile and adult foliage, with the tiny round leaves that are characteristic of seedling and young plants gradually changing over ten years or more to the larger more triangular, slightly lobed leaves more characteristic of *Hibiscus*. The small, single, five-petalled flowers are held upward on the stems, and are borne profusely for much of the year.

Above: The creamy flowers of this rare hibiscus are borne profusely and gradually turn reddish with age.

DOGWOOD AND PROTEA FAMILIES

The dogwoods, Cornaceae, are absent from Australia, and only two genera, Griselinia *and* Corokia, *occur in New Zealand, with the latter often considered to be part of the wider Saxifragaceae group. The proteas (Protaeceae) on the other hand are at their most diverse in Australia, with 42 genera and 860 species, and include flowers of outstanding beauty.*

Drummond's Dryandra

Dryandra drummondii

The dryandras are a large group, closely related to *Banksia*, which show a tremendous variation in form and foliage. This species is restricted to the Swan River area of south-western Australia, where it usually occurs in shallow, poor and clay soils. The leaves form a rosette, in the middle of which is a large flattened, yellow flowerhead, made up of many hundreds of individual flowers. It appears towards the end of the winter.

Identification: A stemless plant with alternate, leathery leaves, 30cm/1ft long and up to 7.5cm/3in broad, incised to the midrib with triangular lobes and densely covered with white down on the underside. The flowerhead is produced at ground level, surrounded by a persistent circle of bracts; the flowers open in succession from the outside in, with the gingery perianths curling back to reveal the yellow styles and stigmas.

Left: Many hundreds of individual flowerheads make up the inflorescence.

Distribution: South-western Australia.
Height and spread: 50–70cm/20–28in.
Habit and form: Rosette-forming shrub.
Leaf shape: Pinnatisect.
Pollinated: Insect or possibly mammal.

Left: All Dryandras are yellow in colour, though the shade of yellow varies considerably.

Saw Banksia

Old man banksia, *Banksia serrata*

This widespread species from eastern Australia is common in sandstone woodland and open forests or sandy soils. It ranges from southern Queensland along the coast to Victoria, with a small population in northern Tasmania, and stretches west as far as the Great Dividing Range. Normally a tree in favourable conditions, its blackened rough bark is a result of surviving many bushfires. The leaves are large and stiff with saw-toothed edges, hence its common name.

Identification: A small tree with knobbly grey bark and leathery, narrowly oval, serrated leaves, 15cm/6in long, glossy dark green above and paler beneath. The flowerheads are dense, terminal, cylindrical spikes, 15cm/6in long, usually greenish-cream, surrounded by a circle of bracts. They appear from summer to autumn and are followed by seed cones with large, protruding follicles.

Left: Seed is usually only released from the cone-like fruits following bush fires.

Distribution: Eastern Australia.
Height and spread: 2–15m/6½–50ft.
Habit and form: Small tree.
Leaf shape: Saw-like.
Pollinated: Birds and possibly insects.

Left: The saw banksia often forms a gnarled, fire-blackened small tree.

Mountain Grevillea

Cat's claw, *Grevillea alpina*

Distribution: South-eastern Australia.
Height and spread: Variable, to 2m/6½ft.
Habit and form: Shrub.
Leaf shape: Linear.
Pollinated: Bird.

Despite its specific name, this plant from south-eastern Australia is a widespread and variable species, occurring at both low and high elevations. It is usually a small shrub with simple rounded leaves, but some forms have much larger leaves with some plants being distinctly hairy. The flowers appear in clusters at the ends of the branches in winter and spring; these too are variable in colour. The species hybridizes naturally with the lavender grevillea, *G. lavandulacea*, and the woolly grevillea, *G. lanigera*, adding to the difficulty of identification.

Identification: A variable, spreading shrub with both prostrate and erect forms. The leaves, up to 2.5cm/1in long, are alternate, narrow to rounded, downy or smooth. The obliquely tubular flowers are borne in short, crowded racemes, paired, in groups of five or seven. Their colours range from greenish-yellow to white, pink-orange and red, and they may be a single colour or a combination.

Below: The tubular flowers have a long, claw-like style.

Far left: The plant usually forms a small shrub.

OTHER DOGWOOD AND PROTEA FAMILY SPECIES OF NOTE

Red Spider Flower *Grevillea punicea*
A native of New South Wales that grows on sandy soils, in heath, open forest or scrubland, often just away from the coast. It is a highly variable species, with bright red flowers from late winter to summer.

Tasmanian Waratah *Telopea truncata*
This upright shrub or small tree grows on moist, acidic soils in wet forest or subalpine scrubland. The young branches and unopened flowerheads are often covered with brownish hairs, the blooms occurring in a loose cluster of red flowers at the ends of the erect stems from late spring to late summer.

Gippsland Waratah *Telopea oreades*
This upright shrub or small tree grows on moist, acidic soils, often alongside creek beds, in wet forest or cool rainforest of southern Victoria, Australia. The red flowers appear in summer. A white form, from the Errinundra Plateau in east Gippsland, is sometimes seen.

New Zealand Privet *Griselinia littoralis*
This fast-growing, evergreen, upright shrub of dense habit bears oval, leathery, bright apple-green leaves, among which the tiny, inconspicuous, yellow-green flowers appear. It is a common hardwood tree throughout the mixed and beech forests of the North, South, and Stewart Islands, from lowland altitudes to subalpine scrub.

Waratah

Telopea speciosissima

The waratah ranges along the central east coast of Australia from sea level to above 1,000m/3,300ft in the Blue Mountains. It grows mainly in the shrub understorey in open forest that has developed on sandstone and adjoining volcanic formations, often on slopes or in gullies. A truly spectacular plant, it is the floral emblem of New South Wales. Its bright red flowers appear in spring and attract the nectar-seeking birds that act as its pollinators.

Identification: A tall, straggling shrub with narrow, leathery, sometimes toothed leaves up to 25cm/10in long. The red flowers are grouped in densely packed, domed terminal racemes up to 15cm/6in wide, surrounded by a circle of large, smooth crimson bracts.

Right: It forms a tall, straggling shrub in time.

Distribution: Central and south-eastern Australia.
Height and spread: 3m/10ft.
Habit and form: Shrub.
Leaf shape: Narrow-obovate.
Pollinated: Bird.

Below: The fruits that develop from mid to late summer contain numerous winged seeds.

Ivory Curl

Buckinghamia celsissima

The rainforests of northern Queensland are the home of this Australian tree, which although rare in the wild, has been widely used as a street tree in Brisbane. It has attractive foliage: the juvenile leaves are often lobed while the new growth is an attractive bronze colour. Its long, curling flowers are white to cream and occur in summer in large racemes that are well displayed at the ends of the branches and are reminiscent of those of grevilleas, as are its fruits.

Left: The fruits contain four seeds.

Identification: A tall, robust, evergreen tree. The juvenile leaves are variable, sometimes lobed; the adult leaves are elliptical, 10–20cm/4–8in long, glossy dark green with conspicuous veins, silver beneath, alternate. The small, creamy-white, scented, tubular flowers have long, slender, curling styles and appear in semi-pendulous, 20cm/8in terminal racemes from summer to late autumn.

Right: The long flower spikes appear at the branch tips.

Far right: Ivory curl forms a very attractive tall tree in its native habitat.

Distribution: North-east Australia.
Height and spread: 30m/100ft.
Habit and form: Tree.
Leaf shape: Elliptic.
Pollinated: Bird.

Long-leaf Lomatia

River lomatia, *Lomatia myricoides*

This Australian species inhabits open forests of eastern New South Wales and Victoria, usually in moist locations such as watercourses, at altitudes up to 1,000m/3,300ft. It is a medium shrub or small tree, with very attractive bark, usually growing tallest in favourable conditions. The scented flowers occur in racemes in the leaf axils or at the ends of branches in summer, and are usually white or cream, although pink forms are known.

Identification: A broadly spreading shrub with ridged young growth, brown and covered in fine hairs, maturing to smooth, grey-brown with branches that are broadly divergent. The narrow leaves are up to 12.5cm/5in long, smooth, tough, mid-green, with margins that may be entire to coarsely toothed at the top half, stalked or stalkless, and variable even on the same plant. Lax racemes up to 15cm/6in long, terminal or axillary at the ends of the branches, appear from spring to summer, produced regularly except during drought; the paired, obliquely tubular flowers are ivory to yellow-green, fragrant and profuse. The flowers are followed by dry fruits containing a number of winged seeds.

Left: The lax racemes of flowers appear at the branch tips during the summer months.

Distribution: South-east Australia.
Height and spread: 2.5m/8ft.
Habit and form: Shrub.
Leaf shape: Linear.
Pollinated: Bird or insect.

Right: The scented flowers occur in racemes.

Right: Lomatia is really a large shrub but in time it can come to resemble a small tree.

Firewheel Tree

White beefwood, *Stenocarpus sinuatus*

Distribution: North-east Australia, Papua New Guinea.
Height and spread: 30m/100ft.
Habit and form: Tree.
Leaf shape: Obovate, lobed.
Pollinated: Bird.

Far right: The firewheel tree is a spectacular sight when in full bloom.

This must surely be one of Australia's most spectacular trees, found in the subtropical and warm temperate rainforests of north-eastern New South Wales and eastern Queensland as well as Papua New Guinea. Its beautiful glossy green leaves and unusual orange-red flowers, shaped like the spokes of a wheel, make it a marvellous sight when it blooms in late summer. The flowers are highly attractive to nectar-feeding birds, appearing near the branch tips in dense umbels in late summer.

Identification: A medium to tall tree with alternate, variable, glossy, dark green leaves, sometimes lobed, or oval to lance-shaped with wavy edges. Terminal, wheel-like umbels 5–7.5cm/2–3in across, consisting of 12–20 narrow red flowers, are produced in the upper leaf axils from summer to autumn. The flowers are followed by woolly grey capsules, containing winged seeds.

OTHER DOGWOOD AND PROTEA FAMILY
SPECIES OF NOTE

Tree Waratah *Alloxylon flammeum*
Native to the rainforest in Queensland, this is a tall tree with glossy green, elliptical leaves, although juvenile leaves may be much larger and lobed. The conspicuous bright red flowers are displayed in the leaf axils towards the ends of the branches in spring and early summer.

Strangea linearis
This small Australian shrub is found in the coastal heaths of north-eastern New South Wales and south-eastern Queensland. It has narrow leaves and small cream flowers, which occur in clusters of two or three in the leaf axils in spring.

Rewarewa *Knightia excelsa*
An upright tree with a slender crown, endemic to New Zealand and found in lowland to montane forest. The small, bright red flowers crowd together to form a bottlebrush-like inflorescence 10cm/4in long.

Guitar Plant
Lomatia tinctoria
An endemic species of open forests and woods of Tasmania, from sea level to 1000m/3,300ft. It is a small shrub with cream or white flowers appearing in summer, in racemes, in the leaf axils, or at the ends of branches. Dry fruits follow, containing winged seeds. Its common name is derived from the shape of the opened fruits.

Grass-leaved Hakea

Hakea multilineata

The gravelly heaths of south-western Australia are home to this large shrub or small tree, whose pink flowers occur in racemes in the leaf axils in winter and spring. Although the flowers occur within the foliage, the plant's open habit means that they are well displayed, never failing to attract attention. The seeds are shed only when stimulated to do so by the occurrence of a bushfire, thereby allowing the seedlings to grow rapidly without competition from other plants.

Distribution: South-western Australia.
Height and spread: 5m/16ft.
Habit and form: Tall shrub or small tree.
Leaf shape: Linear.
Pollinated: Bird, possibly insect.

Identification: A tall shrub or small tree with alternate, grey-green leaves 10–12.5cm/4–5in long, which are rigid to leathery, erect, with 11–15 fine parallel veins. Small, pink-purple, tubular flowers with long, protruding styles appear from midwinter to spring in dense 2.5–7.5cm/2–3in axillary spikes, and are followed by woody seedpods containing two winged seeds.

Right: While it is generally regarded as a large shrub, in time grass-leaved hakea often forms a small, upright tree.

GESNERIAD, ACANTHUS AND JACARANDA FAMILIES

The Gesneriaceae (gesneriads) are mostly tropical herbs and shrubs including well-known ornamental species such as Streptocarpus *and* Gloxinia. *The Acanthaceae (acanthus) are tropical herbs, shrubs or twining vines. The Bignoniaceae (jacarandas) are lianas restricted to the eastern part of Australasia.*

Fieldia

Fieldia australis

This attractive, slightly woody perennial, found in shady spots in the mountains and coastal areas of New South Wales and Victoria, Australia, is actually the sole species in this genus. It forms a tall, climbing shrublet, which clings to mossy bark, especially that of tree ferns, by means of roots that it can put out at need. The large, pure white, tubular flowers arise from spring to summer. When fertilized they eventually turn into large, hanging berries that are white when ripe.

Identification: A tall, climbing subshrub or shrublet often found climbing on tree ferns. The stems, which root as they climb, are red and downy when young, becoming smooth with silvery bark with age. The oval leaves are opposite, of unequal length in each pair, 1.5cm/⅝in or more long, shiny deep green above, paler to silvery below, with downy, reddish midribs, veins and stalks. The large, softly hairy, pure white, pendent, tubular flowers, with a pale green calyx, five petals and white, slightly protruding stamens and stigma, appear singly in the leaf axils. The fruits are large hanging berries, white when ripe, with tiny seeds contained in a fleshy pulp.

Distribution: South-eastern Australia.
Height and spread: 1.8–2.5m/6–8ft.
Habit and form: Climbing subshrub.
Leaf shape: Ovate.
Pollinated: Insect.

New Zealand Gloxinia

Taurepo, waiu-atua, *Rhabdothamnus solandri*

The only African violet genus from New Zealand, this loose, twiggy shrub is found in the coastal forest of North Island, where it favours stream banks. It has rough, hairy leaves that arise from decorative snake-bark stems. The single orange to dark red flowers are carried in succession almost throughout the year, making this one of the prettiest of all New Zealand's forest flowers. The colour of the flowers often pales during the winter.

Identification: A loose, evergreen shrub with purplish young stems and older bark with a snakeskin pattern. The hairy leaves are opposite, oval to elliptical, up to 1cm/⅜in long and coarsely toothed. They are mid- to silvery green with purple veins and spots, on short, purple stalks. The flowers are red-orange with darker stripes or, more rarely, yellow and up to 15mm/⅝in long, arising from the leaf axils. The calyx of five sepals, somewhat reflexed, is purple outside, pale green within and sparsely hairy; the flower is tubular with flared, round lobes; the style and stamens protrude slightly.

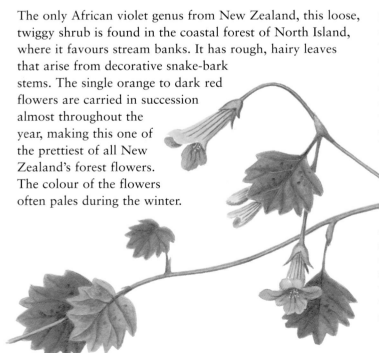

Distribution: New Zealand.
Height and spread: 90–180cm/3–6ft.
Habit and form: Shrub.
Leaf shape: Ovate-elliptical.
Pollinated: Bird.

OTHER GESNERIAD, ACANTHUS AND
JACARANDA FAMILY SPECIES OF NOTE

Cyrtandra pritchardii

This shrub or small tree from Fiji has oval,
toothed leaves and bears white flowers in
axillary cymes throughout most of the year. The
slightly downy flowers are two-lipped, with the
lower lip larger than the upper.

Caricature Plant Graptophyllum pictum

This erect, loosely branched shrub, of obscure
origin, has been widely planted in tropical
gardens and now often exists as an escapee. It
most probably originates from New Guinea, and
is most noted for its glossy, dark green leaves
that are irregularly blotched or marbled.

Bower of Beauty Pandorea jasminoides

This robust, Australian climbing vine reaches up
to the forest canopy in
rainforest from eastern
Victoria to south-east
Queensland. The funnel-
shaped flowers are pale to
deep pink and appear in
terminal clusters from
September to March.

Holly-leaved Fuchsia Graptophyllum ilicifolium

This is a medium shrub with shiny, sharply
toothed leaves. It is native to the lowland rainforests around the Mackay area of Queensland,
Australia. Dense racemes of beautiful, deep red,
tubular flowers are born on short stalks in the
leaf axils in late spring over a short season.

Wonga Wonga Vine

Pandorea pandorana

This vigorous, evergreen climber is found in
habitats from fern gullies to open forest in
Australia, New Guinea and several other
Pacific Islands. It becomes very large over
time as it ascends into the rainforest canopy,
hiding most of its blooms from view. In
spring the vine bears large clusters of small
flowers, variable in hue from white with
purple markings to light red, depending
upon its location.

Identification: An evergreen liana, with a slender
stem and pinnate leaves with six opposite pairs of
glossy, dark
green, lance-
shaped leaflets
up to 10cm/4in
long and 5cm/2in
wide. The leaves
are sparsely glandular
below, entire and
hairless on the upper
surface. The flowers are in
terminal or lateral clusters, up to 20cm/8in long,
often on old wood. They are funnel to bell
shaped, creamy-yellow, and around
2.5cm/1in across, with five short lobes
reflexed to reveal the throats of the flower
that are streaked and splashed red or purple. The
tube is twice the length of the lobes. The beaked,
cylindrical capsule contains winged seeds.

Distribution: Australia, New
Guinea, Pacific Islands.
Height and spread: Up to
30m/100ft.
Habit and form: Liana.
Leaf shape: Pinnate.
Pollinated: Insect.

Scarlet Fuchsia

Graptophyllum excelsum

Distribution: North-east
Australia.
Height and spread:
1.5–8m/5–26ft.
Habit and form: Shrub.
Leaf shape: Spathulate.
Pollinated: Bird.

Found in dry vine thickets, usually on soils
derived from limestone, on the eastern coast
and ranges of Queensland,
Australia, this shrub or
small tree flowers in
spring and early
summer, sporting
many deep red,
tubular blooms
that are borne singly or in pairs
in the leaf axils. In a good
flowering season flowers are borne
in almost every axil, and the
plant becomes a mass of
brilliant scarlet red, which
attracts honeyeaters, probably its
main pollinator. The plants sucker readily
and new clumps appear beside established
plants that can lead to it developing into a
dense thicket in time.

Identification: An erect, evergreen shrub with
multiple stems, often forming large colonies. The
spoon-shaped leaves, 3cm/1¼in long and borne in
opposite pairs, are shiny dark green, with margins
that are mostly smooth, though sometimes toothed,
painted or spotted. The waxy, deep red flowers are
borne on short stalks, often in
great profusion, singly or in
pairs in the leaf axils. They
are tubular, two-lipped and
up to 2.5cm/1in long. The
seed capsules that
follow are club-
shaped, containing
two seeds.

CITRUS FAMILY

There are around 150 genera and 900 species in Rutaceae (the citrus family). They are mostly found in warm to tropical regions and are usually sweet-smelling shrubs or trees. The family produces many edible fruits, some of which, such as oranges, grapefruits and lemons, are important food crops. It displays particular diversity of species in Australasia.

Coastal Correa

Native fuchsia, *Correa backhousiana*

This is a rare plant in the wild, growing only in a limited area in Tasmania and a restricted area of Victoria, Australia. It forms a compact bush, with tubular, pale greenish-yellow flowers from late summer to spring. The leaves have rust-coloured undersides, as do the stems and flower calyces, caused by a woolly covering of small, brown hairy scales, giving the whole plant a very decorative appearance. The plant has become popular in cultivation and may occasionally be encountered far from its native range as a garden escapee.

Identification: A dense, spreading, evergreen shrub with felted, orange-brown stems. The oval, leathery leaves are up to 3cm/1¼in long, with felted brown undersides. The flowers are funnel-shaped, about 2.5cm/1in long, with four lobes, cream to pale green or sometimes orange-brown, axillary or terminal, solitary or in small clusters.

Left: The flowers are a creamy-green colour with calyces covered in a rusty-brown felt.

Right: Correa *forms a compact, slow-spreading, evergreen shrub.*

Distribution: South-east Australia.
Height and spread: 2m/6½ft.
Habit and form: Shrub.
Leaf shape: Ovate.
Pollinated: Insect.

Willow-leaved Crowea

Crowea saligna

The sheltered open forests of the central coastal area of New South Wales are home to this small, pink-flowered shrub. The star-like flowers emerge singly from the leaf axils and are seen over a long season stretching from late summer through to midwinter. The long, thin, willow-like leaves are aromatic. The seeds are naturally dispersed by ants.

Identification: A small shrub, with angular branches and aromatic, lance-shaped leaves up to 8cm/3¼in long, alternately arranged. The star-shaped, five-petalled, pale to mid-pink flowers are produced from the leaf axils or terminally, singly or sometimes paired. They are quite large, with some forms having flowers up to 4.5cm/1¾in in diameter.

Above: The star-like flowers can be variable and are seen here in a rarer white form.

Distribution: Central eastern Australia.
Height and spread: 90cm/3ft.
Habit and form: Shrub.
Leaf shape: Elliptic.
Pollinated: Insect.

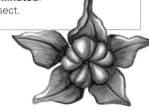

Above and left: The angular branches and aromatic lance-shaped leaves are quite distinctive on this small shrub.

Granite Boronia

Boronia granitica

Distribution: Central eastern Australia.
Height and spread: 90cm/3ft.
Habit and form: Shrub.
Leaf shape: Pinnate.
Pollinated: Insect.

Far right and right: Granite boronia forms a compact evergreen shrub that bears pretty pink flowers over a long period from winter until the early summer.

This medium-sized, compact shrub with pinnate foliage and pink flowers grows in heathy vegetation among granite boulders. It can be found in only a few locations on the north-western side of the New England Tablelands of New South Wales, and the Stanthorpe district of southern Queensland, Australia. It grows either among boulders in the skeletal soils found in narrow rock crevices and fissures, or in adjacent areas on granite scree and shallow soils, in areas of predominantly summer rainfall and cool winters. The flowering season is long, from midwinter to early summer, with the greatest concentration over the spring.

Right: The flowers are followed in late summer and autumn by capsules containing small, black seed that is dispersed by ants.

Identification: An evergreen shrub with opposite, pinnate, aromatic leaves, dotted with glands and covered with hairs. The fragrant flowers are also downy and are pale to bright pink, or occasionally white, with four oval, pointed petals, borne singly from the leaf axils over an extended flowering season from winter to summer.

OTHER CITRUS FAMILY SPECIES OF NOTE
Native Fuchsia *Correa reflexa* var. *cardinalis*
This plant from south-eastern Australia occurs in a variety of habitats, from mountain forests to dry mallee scrub. Its flowers are downy, tubular and yellow-green to crimson, with two or three held together on axillary stalks, appearing mostly between late autumn and late spring.

Phebalium rotundifolium
syn. *Leionema rotundifolium*
This small shrub from open woodland and shrub-land in New South Wales has the clustered, star-shaped, five-petalled, yellow flowers that are typical of the genus, but does not possess the scales on the leaves or stems that are found on many other species.

Diplolaena grandiflora
This striking shrub has oval woolly leaves and pendent red flowers in hairy, green bracts that appear in spring and summer. It is restricted to the south of Western Australia. Although the individual flowers are very small, they are grouped together into large clusters, which may be up to 4cm/1½in across.

White Star *Philotheca myoporoides*
The white star or native daphne comes from open forests and woodlands of Victoria, New South Wales and Queensland, Australia. Its branches are warty and the glossy, deep green leaves have a strong aroma when crushed. From late winter to late spring it is smothered with waxy, white, star-shaped flowers, opening from deep pink buds.

Forest Phebalium

Phebalium squamulosum

This small shrub occurs naturally in open woodland or heath on sandy soils in south-east and north-east Queensland, eastern New South Wales and eastern Victoria, Australia. It is an extremely variable species, with several subspecies and varieties, all of which possess very aromatic foliage and clusters of small, star-like flowers in cream to bright yellow. They appear in early spring. Plants in new leaf have a highly decorative silvery appearance.

Identification: A variable species ranging from slender, small trees to prostrate shrubs. The buds and flowering stalks are covered in small brown scales. The elliptical leaves are bright to grey-green, up to 3cm/1¼in long, sometimes irregularly toothed, and the new growth and undersides of older leaves are covered with silvery scales. The five-petalled flowers appear in early spring and last about four weeks. Though small, they are very conspicuous, occurring in clusters of 12 or more, with cream to yellow pointed petals, bright yellow anthers and long cream stamens.

Right: Forest phebalium is immensely variable, ranging from a small tree to a prostrate shrub.

Distribution: Eastern Australia.
Height and spread: Up to 7m/23ft.
Habit and form: Variable (woody).
Leaf shape: Elliptical.
Pollinated: Insect.

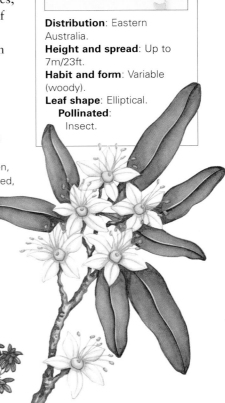

CARNIVOROUS PLANTS

Carnivorous plants have one thing in common: they have evolved the ability to capture and/or digest animals. Over time they have evolved into many forms and often come from diverse ancestry. While some are found in the islands of Oceania, the greatest concentration of species is found in Australia.

Rainbow Plant

Byblis gigantea

This carnivorous plant grows in fire-prone, acid, sandy soils in south-western Australia. It is a close relative of the butterworts, *Punguicula* species, and sundews, *Drosera* species, and its tentacles, much like those of sundews, cover the whole plant, including the stem, leaves and even the flowerheads and buds. Insects are lured to the plants by the sticky mucilage secreted by the stalked glands, which appears to them as dew or nectar. Unlike those of the sundews, the rainbow plant's glands and leaves do not move or curl around their prey.

Identification: A sticky, erect, glandular-hairy, carnivorous herbaceous perennial. The leaves are 10–30cm/4–12in long, narrow and often channelled above, densely sticky and hairy beneath; they have glands with a stem (for trapping insects) and without (for digestion). Flowers up to 4cm/1¾in across appear in summer, growing singly from the axils on hairy stems. They have five overlapping, triangular petals, 2cm/¾in long, and are iridescent blue, pink or purple, with a yellow centre and long, slender style.

Distribution: South-west Australia.
Height and spread: 60cm/2ft.
Habit and form: Perennial herb.
Leaf shape: Linear.
Pollinated: Insect.

Albany Pitcher Plant

Cephalotus follicularis

Found in a small corner of Western Australia, in a 400km/250mile strip from Albany to Eusselton, this curious little plant is the only representative of both its genus and its family, and has no close relatives in the plant kingdom. A variable species in the wild, it produces passive pitcher traps that are mostly used to attract crawling insects: once ensnared they are unable to crawl out of the cleverly designed pods. The traps are produced from spring to autumn and in winter the plant produces small, flat, green leaves. The white flowers are produced on tall, branching stems over the summer.

Identification: A carnivorous herbaceous perennial growing from a short, thick, branched rhizome. The leaves grow in a rosette and are of two kinds: the leaves are 5–7.5cm/2–3in long, oval, rounded, glossy green, often with a red margin; the trapping leaves, which form pitchers up to 5 x 2.5cm/2 x 1in long, are sparsely hairy, green, heavily marked red-brown, with a hinged, ribbed, oval lid attached on the stalk side and three external longitudinal raised nerves swollen into narrow, leaf-like double wings with fringed margins. Small white flowers are borne in terminal panicles on stems up to 60cm/2ft long.

Distribution: Western Australia.
Height and spread: Variable.
Habit and form: Perennial herb.
Leaf shape: Ovate, trapping leaves jug-like.
Pollinated: Insect.

Fairy Aprons

Utricularia dichotoma

Distribution: Australia.
Height and spread: Variable.
Habit and form: Herbaceous perennial.
Leaf shape: Elliptic.
Pollinated: Insect.

This small, Australian, carnivorous herb of permanently wet or seasonally waterlogged soils is only ever likely to be seen when the large, paired, purple flowers appear on long, slender stems. The flower gives the impression of a small skirt, which accounts for the plant's common name. It occurs in all areas of the continent except the Northern Territory, growing from sea level to 1,500m/4,900ft, and flowers year-round, though most commonly in the warmer months.

Identification: A medium-sized, terrestrial, carnivorous herbaceous perennial with numerous, slender, stolons, sometimes fleshy and tuberous. Narrow to broadly elliptic, pointed leaves, up to 14cm/5½in long, grow in rosettes at the nodes. The traps on the stolons are globular to egg-shaped, long-stalked with distinct but variable appendages. The flowers appear on erect stems up to 50cm/20in tall, solitary or in clusters. The flower is two-lipped, with a small, flat upper lip and a larger, semicircular lower lip up to 2.5cm/1in long, dark violet with yellow at the base.

OTHER CARNIVOROUS PLANTS OF NOTE

Utricularia protrusa
This aquatic bladderwort, normally found in slow-moving or still water throughout New Zealand, floats on the surface of the water, with submerged leaves and traps emerging from a long central stem. During winter, resting buds sink, re-emerging in spring. Sulphur-yellow flowers appear from spring to late summer.

Pitcher Plant *Nepenthes mirabilis*
The most widespread species in the genus, this carnivorous pitcher plant, found in northern Australia and much of South-east Asia, occupies a wide range of forest habitats, although always preferring those with a relatively high humidity for much of the year. The plants produce pitchers in various colours, depending upon their place of origin.

Waterwheel Plant *Aldrovanda vesiculosa*
The waterwheel plant is a widespread and curious aquatic, carnivorous herb. It occurs sporadically along the coasts of Queensland, the Northern Territory and far northern Western Australia, as well as in South-east Asia, southern Africa and Europe. It is the only aquatic carnivorous plant with visible trap movement.

Byblis liniflora
This variable, annual carnivorous herb, found in northern Australia and Papua New Guinea, has long, slender leaves with many long-stemmed glands covering much of the plant. The flowers are pink or blue and are produced on long stalks from the leaf axils.

Fork-leaved Sundew

Drosera binata

This robust and variable species is normally found in bogs and swamps, or, in many cases, in roadside drainage ditches. It is very widespread, occurring across Victoria, South Australia, Tasmania, in a small area of south-west Western Australia, and throughout New Zealand. The sticky leaves characteristically divide into two and produce a "tuning fork" shape, and the white (or occasionally pink), sweet-scented blooms are produced between spring and autumn, with the plants usually being dormant from late autumn to early winter.

Distribution: South-eastern Australia, New Zealand.
Height and spread: 50cm/20in.
Habit and form: Perennial herb.
Leaf shape: Forked.
Pollinated: Insect.

Identification: A perennial, rosette-forming, carnivorous herb whose stem is a short rhizome. The variable, basal leaves are erect, on long, usually sparsely hairy, stalks; the blade is deeply cut into 2–14 narrow lobes, with the pointed tip of each lobe furnished with a crown of three or four long tentacles, covered and fringed with gland-tipped hairs above; capable of trapping and digesting insects. Stems up to 50cm/20in long bear many white or pink flowers.

PARASITIC PLANTS

Parasitic plants are found on all continents except Antarctica and the southern oceans are no exception to this. Oceania is the home to an extremely diverse range of parasites, most of which can be gathered together under the general term mistletoes. Mistletoes are only partial parasites, and have green leaves.

Western Australian Christmas Tree

Moodjar, *Nuytsia floribunda*

This bush is a native of sandy or granite soil in open forest, woodland and heath in Western Australia. It is related to the mistletoe and is, at least in the early stages of its life, dependent on a host plant. When its roots encounter those of another plant, they form a collar-like "haustorium", a structure that cuts into the host root to extract nutrients and moisture. The species famously flowers at around Christmas time, when its bright yellow flowers, borne in clusters at the end of the branches, make the whole plant a spectacular, seasonal highlight.

Right:
The bright yellow flowers appear on branch tips around Christmas time.

Identification: An evergreen shrub or small tree with rough, grey-brown bark, which parasitizes the roots of grasses as much as 50m/160ft away. The leaves are 2.5–10cm/1–4in long, opposite, subopposite or occasionally whorled, lance-shaped with pointed or rounded tips, narrowing at the base. The brilliant orange-yellow flowers appear in large, crowded terminal clusters over several months. The fruit is brown, dry and three-winged, with sticky seeds.

Distribution: Western Australia.
Height and spread: 7m/23ft.
Habit and form: Shrub or small tree.
Leaf shape: Lanceolate.
Pollinated: Insect.

Rosewood Mistletoe

Amyema scandens

This showy mistletoe species is native to the moist tropical forests of Papua New Guinea, New Caledonia and Borneo, with a few isolated occurrences on the Australian east coast, where it is a parasite of the rosewood tree, *Dalbergia sissoo*. The species grows at elevations from sea level to 1,600m/5,200ft in both primary and secondary rainforest and in open humid forests, on a wide range of hosts. It is a variable species, with red or pink tubular flowers appearing close to the branches of the host.

Identification: A semi-parasitic shrub, with external runners and robust stems, with distinct lenticels, enlarged at the nodes. The elliptic to circular leathery leaves are mostly in whorls of five to eight, or rarely four; they are very variable, lance-shaped to oval, up to 20cm/8in long, sometimes with wavy margins. The clusters of slender, stemless red or pink flowers appear at the nodes and on the runners.

Distribution: Papua New Guinea, New Caledonia, Borneo.
Height and spread: Variable.
Habit and form: Semi-parasitic shrub.
Leaf shape: Lanceolate to ovate.
Pollinated: Insect.

Left: Amyema scandens *is an endangered species of parasite.*

New Zealand Red Mistletoe

Peraxilla tetrapetala

This mistletoe, endemic to New Zealand, has showy, bright red flowers, and is most commonly seen on mountain beech, *Nothofagus* species, and tawheowheo trees, *Quintinia* species, in the forests of North Island and also on silver beech, *N. menziesii*, on South Island. It is most frequently found on the inner branches and the host trunk, where the flowers provide a dazzling display in early summer. It has the distinction of being the only plant in the world with bird-pollinated explosive flowers, which are also opened by insects.

Identification: Semi-parasitic, bushy shrub, joined to its host by several haustoria (attachments). The rhombic leaves are oppositely arranged on short stalks and are thick and fleshy, usually with some blisters on the surface caused by gall-forming insects. The flowers are tubular in bud, with a clubbed tip, and have four petals, red or yellow at the base shading gradually to crimson at the reflexed tips, and protruding stamens and stigma. The fruit is a greenish-yellow, semi-translucent drupe, appearing in autumn.

Distribution: New Zealand.
Height and spread: 90cm/3ft.
Habit and form: Semi-parasitic shrub.
Leaf shape: Rhombic.
Pollinated: Insect.

Right: The fruits of the New Zealand red mistletoe are dull green.

OTHER PARASITIC PLANT SPECIES OF NOTE

Dendrophthoe acacioides
This aerial stem-parasite from the Northern Territory and Western Australia has conspicuous orange flowers, held on axillary spikes, which adorn the sparsely leafed runners. The mature bud is usually inflated and curved with the open, star-like flower.

Decaisnina signata
This mistletoe is found mainly on *Barringtonia*, *Planchonia* and *Ficus* trees in the monsoon forest of the Northern Territory. It has showy, orange, tubular flowers with yellow-and-black lobes, arranged in terminal spikes.

Yellow Beech Mistletoe *Alepis flavida*
The yellow beech mistletoe is a native of both North Island and South Island of New Zealand, where it mostly occupies mountain or black beech, *Nothofagus* species, as a host. It has small, orange-yellow to yellow flowers in summer, followed by shiny, golden-yellow berries.

Daenikera corallina
This monotypic genus occurs only in the dense wet forests of New Caledonia, where it is parasitic on the roots or trunk bases of forest trees. The new growth is bright red, becoming brown with age. Tiny burgundy flowers are followed by red fruits that turn blue with age.

Galapagos Dwarf Mistletoe

Phoradendron henslowii

This mistletoe, seen on trees on Santa Cruz and Isabella Island, Galapagos, is an endemic species that grows in the elevated cloud forest vegetation of those islands. It is related to other dwarf mistletoes, whose principal centre of diversity is in Mexico and the western United States, and in some respects it resembles the Ecuadorian species *P. nervosum*. The oval, leathery leaves are paired and joined at their bases, and the small, greenish flowers on thin red spikes give rise to small, pinky-white berries.

Identification: A semi-parasitic shrub, with green stems and reddish buds and nodes, with a dense or sparse growth habit, often forming an extensive colony within the host canopy. The variable, waxy, oval leaves are smooth, pale green, often with darker margins, becoming mottled darker and with red spots with age. The small, greenish flowers and greyish, sticky berries are held terminally on the branchlets, subtended by paired leaves.

Distribution: Santa Cruz and Isabella Island, Galapagos.
Height and spread: Variable.
Habit and form: Semi-parasitic shrub.
Leaf shape: Obovate.
Pollinated: Insect.

Left: Dwarf mistletoe grows only on trees in cloud forest regions.

Below: The small, greyish berries appear on the branch tips on red stems.

DUCKWEED, ARUM AND GINGER FAMILIES

Lemnaceae, the duckweed family, is widespread across Australia. The Araceae, arum family, are rhizomatous or tuberous herbs characterized by an inflorescence that is a fleshy spadix partially enveloped by a bract or spathe. The Zingiberaceae (ginger family) are perennial herbs, mostly with creeping horizontal or tuberous rhizomes. They have a wide distribution, mainly in the tropics.

Taro

Coco yam, *Colocasia esculenta*

This plant is grown as a crop for its edible corms and leaves throughout the humid tropics and is used in Africa, Asia, the West Indies and South America. Its origins are very obscure: it is probably a selection of an ancestral wild food. It was extremely important to the Polynesian, Melanesian and Micronesian peoples, who transported it across the Pacific Ocean, where it occurs as an introduced vagrant on many islands. It is most recognizable for its large, arrow-shaped leaves, the flowers being rather insignificant and rarely setting viable seed.

Identification: A perennial herb with thick shoots from a large corm; slender stolons are also often produced, along with offshoot corms. The leaf blades, up to 60cm/24in long and 50cm/20in wide, are arrow-shaped, with a dark green, velvety upper surface; the leaf stalks, which join the middle of the leaf, are succulent and often purplish near the top. The inflorescence is a yellow spathe 20–40cm/8–16in long, surrounding a spadix 5–15cm/2–6in, on a stout stem; the flowers are tiny and densely crowded on the upper stalk, female flowers below, male flowers above. The fruits are small berries in clusters on the stalk, producing few seeds, which are rarely viable.

Distribution: Pan-tropical.
Height and spread: 1.5m/5ft.
Habit and form: Herbaceous perennial.
Leaf shape: Sagittate.
Pollinated: Unclear, rarely sets seed.

Above: The corm is an important food crop.

Right: The leaves are quite distinctive.

Star Duckweed

Ivy leaf duckweed, *Lemna trisulca*

This diminutive, floating, aquatic perennial is found throughout the world's temperate zones in both hemispheres, where it often forms tangled masses just under the water surface. The leaves and stems are merged in a common structure that usually has a single root below. It is distinguished from other *Lemna* species by the stalked fronds that aggregate into chains. The tiny flowers, although uncommon, occur on small fronds with toothed margins, which rise to float on the surface.

Identification: A minute, aquatic herb, floating just below the water surface, consisting of a leaf-like frond and a single root. Fronds 3–15mm/⅛–⅝in long and up to 5mm/⅛in wide, submerged except when flowering, narrow at the base to form a 3–20mm/⅛–¾in-long stalk, cohering and often forming branched chains with margins toothed at the base. The roots (sometimes not developed) are up to 2.5cm/1in long, with pointed rootcaps. Flowers and fruits are rare.

Above and right: The tiny leaf-like stems of this floating, aquatic plant reproduce rapidly and can form a dense "carpet" across the surface in favourable conditions.

Right: The microscopic flowers of this unusual plant are hardly ever seen.

Distribution: Cosmopolitan.
Height and spread: Spread indefinite.
Habit and form: Aquatic herb.
Leaf shape: N/A.
Pollinated: Water.

Pinecone Ginger

Shampoo ginger, *Zingiber zerumbet*

This widespread plant, believed to originate from India and the Malaysian Peninsula, is an example of a species so long under cultivation in so many places throughout the Pacific and Oceania that it is uncertain where it originated, although it was widely introduced by Polynesian settlers. It develops conical bracts, resembling pinecones, which produce creamy-yellow flowers. The bracts contain a clear soapy liquid that has been used by Polynesians to wash the hair and skin, and all its parts are spicily fragrant.

Distribution: Austronesian and Pacific regions.
Height and spread: 2m/6½ft.
Habit and form: Herbaceous perennial.
Leaf shape: Lanceolate.
Pollinated: Insect or bird.

Right: The tall stems arise from an underground rhizome, with flower and leaf stems borne separately.

Far right: The creamy-yellow flowers appear from the tight flower cones.

Identification: A tall, perennial herb with branching, thick, aromatic rhizomes and leafy, reed-like stems. The leaves, which are arranged in two ranks, are lance-shaped, up to 35cm/14in long, closely set, smooth above and hairy beneath. Separate flower stalks 20–45cm/8–18in tall arise in mid- to late summer, bearing pale green, cone-shaped bracts, which gradually turn red. Creamy-yellow, three-petalled, tubular flowers, about 3cm/1¼in long, appear on the cones.

OTHER DUCKWEED, ARUM AND GINGER FAMILY SPECIES OF NOTE

Chinese Evergreen *Aglaonema commutatum*
The inappropriately named Chinese evergreen is actually a native of the Philippines and north-east Celebes. It has been widely planted as an ornamental elsewhere and often persists as an escapee. It is an evergreen perennial with elliptical, dark green, silver mottled leaves and creamy-white axillary flowers enclosed by a pale green spathe.

Stinky Lily *Typhonium brownii*
The aptly named stinky lily grows on rainforest margins, in sheltered gullies and along creek banks from coastal New South Wales and up into Queensland, Australia. It gains its name by virtue of the smell of the newly opened flowers, which, when they open on summer evenings, smell strongly of excrement.

Red Ginger *Guillainia purpurata*
Commonly grown in tropical gardens and possibly a native of South-east Asia, although it has been widely cultivated, red ginger is now naturalized in many tropical islands. The attractive, brilliant red inflorescences consist of large, waxy bracts with small, white, inconspicuous flowers inside.

Amorphophallus glabra
From New Guinea and tropical northern Australia, where it grows principally in lowland forest areas, this plant has a cylindrical, green spathe enclosing a green spadix, held on top of a long scape above the foliage.

White Ginger Lily

Hedychium coronarium

This showy plant, probably a native of eastern India, was transported around the Pacific by Polynesian settlers and is frequently cultivated and naturalized in tropical island forests. The stalks are topped with long clusters of wonderfully fragrant white flowers that look like butterflies. The flowers are popular in Hawaii and the Pacific Islands, where they are used in leis or worn singly in the hair or behind the ear.

Identification:
An erect, perennial herb with stout rhizomes and numerous reed-like stems. The lance-shaped, pointed leaves, 60cm/24in long and 10cm/4in wide, are arranged in two ranks, stemless or on short stems. The very fragrant flowers are borne in summer in dense spikes 15–30cm/6–12in long, with two to six flowers per bract. They have three petals and are white with a yellow-green centre. They eventually give way to showy seedpods full of bright red seeds.

Distribution: Eastern India and Pacific regions.
Height and spread: Up to 3m/10ft.
Habit and form: Perennial herb.
Leaf shape: Lanceolate.
Pollinated: Insect or bird.

Above: The large, flowers appear at the branch tips.

Left: The leafy stems arise from underground rhizomes.

IRIS AND AMARYLLIS FAMILIES

Iridaceae, the iris family, are mostly perennial herbs from rhizomes, bulbs or corms which occur in both tropical and temperate regiosn. The flowers commonly occur at the top of a branched or unbranched stem, each with sex petals in two rings of three. Amaryllicaceae, the amaryllis family, are perennial herbs from a bulb with contractile roots. The flower usually consists of six distinct or fused petaloid tepals.

Darling Lily

Macquarie lily, Murray lily, *Crinum flaccidum*

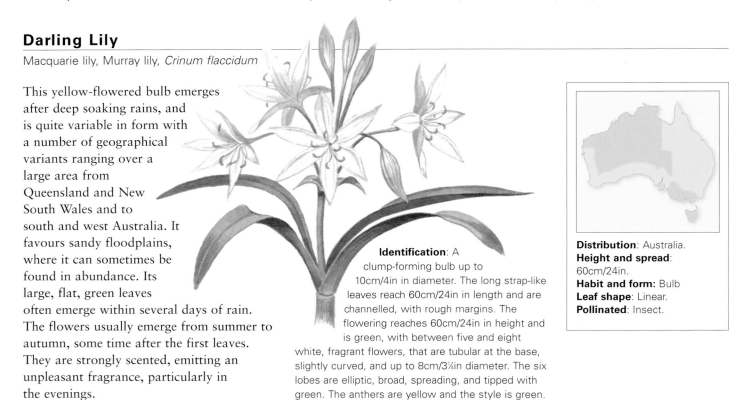

This yellow-flowered bulb emerges after deep soaking rains, and is quite variable in form with a number of geographical variants ranging over a large area from Queensland and New South Wales and to south and west Australia. It favours sandy floodplains, where it can sometimes be found in abundance. Its large, flat, green leaves often emerge within several days of rain. The flowers usually emerge from summer to autumn, some time after the first leaves. They are strongly scented, emitting an unpleasant fragrance, particularly in the evenings.

Identification: A clump-forming bulb up to 10cm/4in in diameter. The long strap-like leaves reach 60cm/24in in length and are channelled, with rough margins. The flowering reaches 60cm/24in in height and is green, with between five and eight white, fragrant flowers, that are tubular at the base, slightly curved, and up to 8cm/3¼in diameter. The six lobes are elliptic, broad, spreading, and tipped with green. The anthers are yellow and the style is green.

Distribution: Australia.
Height and spread: 60cm/24in.
Habit and form: Bulb
Leaf shape: Linear.
Pollinated: Insect.

Silky Purple Flag

Patersonia sericea

This iris-like perennial herb is widespread from north-eastern Victoria to south-eastern Queensland. It thrives in grassland, woodland and open forest, and is one of the most commonly encountered species of the genus. The three-petalled flowers occur mostly in the spring, on grey woolly stems, which are shorter than the leaves. The flowers are deep purple-blue, often closing before noon in hot, sunny weather. Before opening, the flowers are enclosed in two large, papery bracts and although each flower only opens for a single day, new flowers are produced over an extended period.

Identification: A perennial herb ascending from a short rhizome with stems to 30cm /12in, which are covered with silky, woolly hairs. The leaves are linear, erect, stiff, woolly at the base when young, clustered at the base of the stem, evenly and oppositely arranged, usually forming a fan. The inflorescence consists of a few- to several-flowered, sessile spikes enclosed in spathes: each spikelet being several-flowered. The flowers are regular, short-lived, deep violet-blue, with a slender perianth tube. The outer tepals are broadly ovate, woolly when young, while the inner tepals are lanceolate or ovate and rather small by comparison.

Distribution: Eastern Australia.
Height and spread: 30cm/1ft.
Habit and form: Perennial herb.
Leaf shape: Linear.
Pollinated: Insect.

Swamp Iris

Patersonia fragilis

Distribution: Eastern Australia.
Height and spread: 30cm/1ft.
Habit and form: Perennial herb.
Leaf shape: Linear.
Pollinated: Insect.

Found in the eastern states of Australia, from Queensland down to Tasmania and across to South Australia, this tussock-forming plant is often found associated with tea tree heath, particularly on moist ground. It flowers from September to January and looks like an iris, with purple flowers and a rhizomatous root system. The greyish-green twisted leaves are often longer than the flower stem and obscures the blooms from view until seen from almost above, making this an easy plant to miss when among other vegetation.

Identification: A herbaceous perennial with a short rhizome from which stems grow to 30cm/1ft or more. The leaves, to 45cm/18in long, are often longer than the flower stem. They are greyish-green, twisted, clustered at the base of the stem, linear and usually forming a fan or tussocky mass. The inflorescence is a several-flowered sessile spike, enclosed in a spathe; the bracts are scarious; the flowers are regular, short-lived and purple. The outer three tepals are broad and spreading; the inner three are erect and small, forming an enclosing sheath around the stamens and style.

OTHER IRIS AND AMARYLLIS SPECIES OF NOTE

Yellow Flag Flower *Patersonia xanthina*
This rhizomatous, west Australian species has bright buttercup-yellow, three-petalled flowers that appear in the spring among a loose mass of thin, grass-like foliage, in open woodland and heath on sandy soils. A striking and easily recognizable species.

Purple Flag *Patersonia occidentalis*
This tall, free-flowering species occurs naturally in south-western Australia, flowering in spring to reveal a mass of purple, three-petalled, iris-like flowers among the grassy tussock of foliage, which often continue appearing over a long period until the early summer. Colour is blue to purple.

Spider Lily *Crinum asiaticum*
This large coarse herb is found throughout the tropical Indo-Pacific. The stout stems bear leaves and inflorescences in a crown at their apex, often with 25–30 flowers in each one. The white flowers, with rich purple filaments and yellow anthers are very decorative.

Swamp Lily *Crinum pedunculatum*, Spider lily, River lily, St John's lily
Native to Australia, the swamp lily is probably a variant of *C. asiaticum*, which has adapted to subtropical conditions ranging as far south as the Hunter River in New South Wales. The white, scented flowers occur in heads, similar to those of *C. asiaticum* but are generally a little more compact.

Orange Libertia

Mikoikoi, *Libertia peregrinans*

This flower is found in moist grassy areas and scrub on the west coast of New Zealand's North Island, between Kawhia and Wellington, and from a few locations on South Island and nearby coastal islands. It has strap-like, tufted, veined leaves that turn an attractive orange colour in cool weather. The flowers, which resemble a small iris, are white, star-shaped with yellow anthers, and are produced in spring. Burnt-orange, marble-sized seedpods follow the flowers.

Distribution: New Zealand.
Height and spread: To 70cm/28in.
Habit and form: Herbaceous perennial .
Leaf shape: Linear.
Pollinated: Insect.

Identification: This plant consists of leafy fans, which emerge at intervals from horizontal stolons. The leaves are 13–70cm/5–28in long, 1cm/⅜in wide, and are copper-coloured. They are many-veined with the median ones crowded and coloured red or orange. The flowers and fruits are carried below the leaves. The panicles of flowers are narrow, closely branched, with long lower bracts and shorter upper bracts. Each has one to seven flowers per branch. The flowers are to 2.5cm/1in in diameter; with bright white tepals that are oblong-elliptical or oblong. The anthers are dark yellow-brown. The seedpod is an ovoid-barrel-shape.

WATER LILIES, BUCK BEANS, LOTUS LILIES, PICKERELWEEDS AND APONOGETON

Aquatic plants often have immensely showy flowers, and include among their number species considered as the most basally "primitive" of the flowering plants. They all live in a challenging environment and show a variety of ingenious solutions to the problem of survival.

Giant Water Lily

Nymphaea gigantea

This waterlily, native to north Australia and New Guinea is quite scarce, occurring in lagoons and slow-flowing creeks, in deep soft mud. It is a magnificent species with large blooms held high above the water, which emerge and are best seen in the day. Their abundant yellow stamens are very striking and both white- and pink-petalled variants can be found as well as the more common blue form.

Identification: An aquatic herbaceous perennial with tuberous roots. The leaves are to 60cm/2ft in diameter, ovate to orbicular, glabrous, green above, green tinged pink to purple beneath. The base of each is deeply cleft into two-lobes, with the lobes often overlapping. The margins are finely dentate. The petioles are usually elongate, glabrous. The flowers, to 30cm/1ft diameter, are sky-blue to blue-purple, scentless, opening in the day and closing at night. The sepals are ovate to elliptic, green, with the margins and exterior surface often blue. The 18–50 petals are obovate enclosing 350–750 stamens, which are bright yellow. The fruit is berry-like, maturing under water. The seeds have a floating aril.

Distribution: North Australia and south New Guinea.
Height and spread: Variable.
Habit and form: Aquatic, perennial herb.
Leaf shape: Rounded.
Pollinated: Insect, usually beetles.

Left: The large blooms are held high above the water and rounded, green leaves.

Water Snowflake

Nymphoides indica

This pretty, fast-growing, perennial water plant, has an extremely wide tropical distribution, inhabiting pools, pans, marshes and rivers throughout Australia and New Zealand, as well as southern and tropical Africa, India and Asia. Although it bears some resemblance to water lilies, it is not related. It has flat, rounded, floating leaves, and floating stems that form tufted plantlets along their lengths. The delicate, white flowers with yellow centres, have unusual, feathery-edged petals and mostly appear between October and May.

Identification: An aquatic perennial herb with creeping rhizomes and elongated stems that form tufted plantlets along their length. Roots form at the nodes, particularly in seasons of drought. The floating leaves, to 15cm/6in in diameter, but usually far smaller, are orbicular, pale glossy green, long-stalked, deeply cordate at the base, with margins that are entire or undulate. The flowers are borne in profusion from October until May, emerging ephemeral, on slender stalks arising from petioles. The petals to 1cm/⅜in, are white, stained deep yellow at the centre, and are covered in white glandular hairs or are densely papillose. Petal margins are fringed. Each flower has five stamens inserted at the base of the corolla. The stigma is bifid and the ovary is single-celled. The fruit is a capsule.

Distribution: Australia, New Zealand, Africa, India, Asia.
Height and spread: Variable.
Habit and form: Aquatic, perennial herb.
Leaf shape: Rounded.
Pollinator: Insect.

Below: The unusual feathery flowers appear around the leaves.

Sacred Bean

Nelumbo nucifera

Distribution: Australia, Asia.
Height and spread: Variable.
Habit and form: Aquatic, herbaceous perennial.
Leaf shape: Rounded.
Pollinated: Insect.

This striking Australian native perennial can be found across much of Asia. Its floating and emergent, blue-green leaves can be found in stationary or slow-moving water in lagoons and floodplain watercourses, mostly in tropical zones. It is a spectacular sight when in bloom. The soft pink blossom opens on top of a stiff stalk, which emerges from below the water. The easily recognized, large fruit structure develops as the flower opens and turns brown when the flower fades and the petals fall into the water. It is prized by florists for use in dried arrangements.

Left: The soft pink blooms appear above the water on long stems.

Identification: A perennial aquatic herb with a spongy, horizontal and wide-spreading rhizome. The leaves are long-petiolate, to 2m/6½ft above the surface, to 80cm/32in across. They are glaucous, with a margin that is undulate peltate and veins that radiate. The flowers are solitary, emerging from the water, large and showy, pink or white, very fragrant, to 30cm/1ft diameter. Each has four or five green sepals and numerous petals that are arranged spirally. A mass of 200–400 stamens, to 12.5 x 7.5cm/5 x 3in, each have yellow anthers. The 2cm/¾in fruits provide ellipsoid seeds, which can survive for hundreds of years in river mud.

OTHER SPECIES OF NOTE

Yellow Water Snowflake *Nymphoides crenata*
This pretty perennial water plant has yellow flowers with five characteristically fringed petals, held above the heart-shaped leaves. The leaves arise from a stoloniferous base, floating on the water surface, and the floating runners produce new plants along their length.

Blue Lily *Nymphaea violacea*
The blue lily is a showy aquatic plant from northern Australia, which can be seen along the margins of billabongs. It has large, round, floating leaves and bears violet-tipped, white flowers that appear between January and July, on long stalks up to 30cm/ 12in above the water surface.

Queensland Lace Plant *Aponogeton elongatus*
This pondweed, native to north and eastern Australia is found in the shallow turnings of slow-flowing rivers. It has long, wavy-edged, mostly submerged or occasionally floating leaves, and a yellow, usually simple flower spike that emerges in the summer.

Cobooree *Aponogeton queenslandicus*
This rare water plant, occurs in Queensland, the Northern Territory and the far west of New South Wales, Australia. It is threatened by invasive introduced grass species. It has lance shaped floating leaves and bright lemon-yellow floating spikes of flowers.

Bog Hyacinth

Monochoria cyanea

The billabongs, swamps and, small watercourses of northern Australia are the home of this attractive plant, which generally likes to grow rooted in soft muddy sediments. It begins life as a floating-leaved plant, which in time changes to the adult form with a loose rosette of rounded leaves. The short flower stems appear to emerge from the leaf stalk, and each one produces several pretty blue to purple flowers in the summer.

Distribution: North Australia.
Height and spread: Variable.
Habit and form: Aquatic, annual or perennial herb.
Leaf shape: Ovate.
Pollinated: Insect.

Identification: An annual or perennial aquatic herb with a short, creeping rhizome and short erect stems. The leaves emerge on long petioles, basal or alternate on the stem. They are cordate-ovate to lanceolate in shape. The inflorescence has a solitary, terminal, sheathing leaf enclosing a membranous spathe at the base of stalk. The spathe shape is variable, sometimes with the lower spathe enclosing the upper. The flowers appear in elongated racemes. The outer flower appears in six sections. It is tubular to oblong, blue, often spotted red, with six stamens, with oblong anthers; one large and blue, the other five smaller and yellow. The fruit capsule has numerous seeds.

GRASSES AND SEDGES

The Poaceae, more commonly known as grasses, are mostly herbaceous perennials, comprising one of the largest and, from the point of view of human and grazing animals, most important families of flowering plants with about 500 genera and 8,000 species. The Cyperaceae (sedges) are grass-like, herbaceous plants comprising about 70 genera and 4,000 species, commonly found in wet or saturated conditions.

Rice Sedge

Dirty Dora, *Cyperus exaltatus*

This tussock-forming, grass-like plant is a common sight in the freshwater wetlands of much of Australia, where it thrives on riverbanks, creekbanks, frequently inundated alluvial floodplains, drainage channels, lagoons and shallow dams. Superficially. the plant resembles grasses, but its green stems are a distinctive triangular shape. The reddish-brown spikes of flowers appear in summer, autumn or winter, depending upon the location they are found in.

Far left: The stems of rice sedge are three-sided, making them quite distinctive and easy to identify.

Identification: Rice sedge is a robust, tussock-forming, aquatic perennial, to 2m/6½ft tall. The leaves are 5–15mm/³⁄₁₆–⅝in wide. The culms are triangular and smooth, 1–1.8m (39–72in) high, to 8mm (⅜in) diameter. The inflorescence is compound or decompound, with five to ten primary branches to 18cm/7in long. The spikes are narrow-cylindrical, 2–5cm/⅘–5in long, and 5–15mm/³⁄₁₆–⅝in diameter. The four to six bracts surrounding the inflorescence are leaf-like, to 90cm/3ft long. The flattened spikelets, which are numerous per spike, to 2cm/¾in long, with 6–44 flowers appear in spring and summer. The fruit is a yellow-brown, ellipsoid nut.

Distribution: Widespread in tropics and warm climates.
Height and spread: 2m/6½ft.
Habit and form: Tussock-forming aquatic perennial.
Leaf shape: Linear.
Pollinated: Wind.

Left: The seeds, held tightly in the spikelets are small nuts that are easily borne by water.

River Club Rush

Schoenoplectus tabernaemontani (syn. *Schoenoplectus validus*)

This stout, grass-like perennial species occurs across a very wide range, including the Americas, Eurasia, Africa, many Pacific Islands as well as Australia and New Zealand. It grows in both fresh and brackish marshes, tidal shores, shallow margins of ponds, quiet waters and on some riverbanks. It is an extremely variable plant that is probably really a cluster of very closely related subspecies, all of which hybridize freely. The erect, soft, circular flowering stems have only small leaves and are topped by small clusters of drooping flowers covered by red-brown spiral, scales.

Identification: An erect perennial standing 90cm–3m/3–10ft tall. It is semi-aquatic, and often forms large colonies. It has spongy cylindrical, bluish-green stems with big air chambers. The roots develop from a shallow rhizome, to 1cm/⅖in diameter. Each stem produces three or four, basal leaves that are often pinnate-fibrillose; margins often scabridulous. The inflorescences is branched, each with two to four branches to 20cm/8in long. The 15–200 spikelets are solitary or in clusters of two to four, but most commonly all are solitary. Each scale is uniformly dark to pale orange-brown, sometimes straw-coloured. The fruiting time is variable according to location, but is usually in spring to summer.

Distribution: Widespread across the world.
Height and spread: 90–300cm/3–10ft.
Habit and form: Erect, semi-aquatic perennial.
Leaf shape: Linear.
Pollinator: Wind.

Left: The small clusters of drooping flowers can be variable according to where the plant grows.

Salt Couch

Sand couch, *Sporobolus virginicus*

This rhizomatous, perennial grass species occurs widely from Australia and New Zealand to the Pacific Islands, West Indies, Africa, India, China and Indonesia; mostly inhabiting salt marshes and sand hills. Its long thin, paired, spine-tipped and wiry leaf-blades emerge in erect clusters from the underground rhizomes looking like individual plants from which the dense pale flower spikes emerge.

Right: The small pale flowers emerge when it is warm.

Far right: In time the spreading habit of the plant results in dense wiry clumps.

Identification: This prostrate or almost erect perennial grass grows up to 40cm/16in high. The underground parts consist of stout creeping horizontal stems with scales. It produces vegetative and flowering shoots that arise singly from the underground stems and branching above. The lower leaves remain undeveloped, arising as shining pale sheaths. The upper leaves are arranged in two opposite rows. They are finely grooved, with blades to 7cm/2¾in long, inrolled, and rigid. The plant's stems are circular in cross-section, smooth and branched. The seedhead, to 6cm/2¼in long, projects from or is enclosed in the uppermost leaf sheath. It is lead-coloured. Spikelets of flowers, to 2.5mm/¹⁄₁₆in long, appear in the warmer months in more temperate regions, but the plant is able to produce seed several times a year in tropical regions.

Distribution: Australia, New Zealand, Pacific Islands, West Indies, Africa, Asia.
Height and spread: 40cm/16in.
Habit and form: Perennial grass.
Leaf shape: Linear.
Pollinator: Wind.

OTHER SPECIES OF NOTE

Variable Flatsedge *Cyperus difformis*
Also known as small-flower umbrella plant, this is a fast-growing, erect, annual sedge, widespread across much of Australia and Oceani,a and a common weed of rice fields. It is well adapted to moist lowland soils or flooded areas. The small, rounded flowerheads appear near the top of the stems.

Spike Rush *Eleocharis equisetina*
Grown in parts of Asia for its edible corms and native down as far south as northeastern Australia in marshy land and the edges of seasonal swamps. The tube-shaped, leafless, brittle, sharply pointed, erect, green stems, have flowers in spikelets near their tops.

Kangaroo Grass *Themeda triandra* (syn. *Themeda australis*)
An easily recognized, tussock-forming grass, with unusual flower and seedheads, found in all warm and tropical regions of the Old World. Once the dominant grass in much of Australia, introduced livestock has reduced the populations.

Weeping Grass *Microlaena stipoides*
Arguably Australia's most important native grass, with a widespread distribution stretching beyond the continent, mostly in high rainfall areas. It has slender, weeping seedheads, and a variable, growth habit from prostrate to erect, according to its location.

Oryza australiensis

This species of rice is found in the tropical regions of northern Australia where it naturally inhabits undulating plains of *Eucalyptus* and grasslands or in box woodland; mostly in wet places such as swamps, the edges of freshwater lagoons, seasonally dry pools, alluvial streams, or behind river levees. The loose, open, wispy flowerheads, are initially pale green, turning a straw colour as the dry season progresses, yielding a small rice grain upon ripening.

Identification: A perennial, rhizomatous grass, to 2m/6½ft or more in height, which stands erect and is robust. The leaves are strap-shaped to linear, and flat. They have a papery quality and are grey-green or dark-green. The inflorescence is a panicle that is loose and open. The spikelets are pear-shaped 8mm/⅝in long and 2.5mm/¹⁄₁₀in wide, laterally compressed and three-flowered.

Right: The loose open flowerhead contains numerous rounded seeds that are similar to cultivated rice grains.

Distribution: North Australia.
Height and spread: 2m/78in.
Habit and form: Perennial grass.
Leaf shape: Linear.
Pollinator: Wind.

Below: The wispy flowerheads arre drooping and green when young.

LILIES, ANTHERIAS, ASPARAGES AND ASPHODELS

Lilies (Liliaceae), asphodels (Asphodelaceae), antherias (Anthericaceae) and asparages (Asparagaceae)
were all formerly classed together and share many similarities. Most of them have extremely showy
flowers and they are well represented across the whole of Australasia and Oceania.

Fringe Lily

Thysanotus multiflorus

This very striking plant from the southern tip of western Australia is found in a range of mostly dry habitats from forest to coastal plain sands. It has a clump of grass-like leaves that are rarely noticed among other grasses until the delicate mauve flowers appear in summer. Each of the three petals has frilly edges and while the individual flowers only last a day, the plant continues to produce flowers over several months, making this one of the most noticeable flowers at this time.

Identification: A rhizomatous perennial with simple, naked stems. The leaves are linear, grass-like and expanded into papery, sheathing wings at the base. Each plant produces 3–30 linear to narrowly lanceolate leaves, 20–30cm/8–12in long, sometimes channelled, glabrous with margins entire. The scapes are erect, glabrous, 15–30cm/6–12in. The inflorescence is a solitary umbel containing 4–20 or more blue-violet flowers. The six perianth segments are 6–20mm/¼–¾in long, with outer segments linear to narrowly oblanceolate, to 2.5mm/⅒in wide, inner segments to 8mm/⅜in wide. Each has three stamens, with twisted filaments, and purple to yellow anthers.

Distribution: Western Australia.
Height and spread: 20–30cm/8–12in.
Habit and form: Rhizomatous perennial.
Leaf shape: Linear (grass-like).
Pollinated: Insect.

Poor Knights Lily

Xeronema callistemon

This unusual, but highly decorative, plant found only on inaccessible inland cliff areas of the Poor Knights Islands is situated off the northeast coast of New Zealand. It forms a clump of sword-shaped, green leaves and has unusual bottlebrush flower clusters that grow horizontally, like a giant, red toothbrush. The stunning red flowers emerge straight up from the stalk and have bright orange pollen. Another species (*Xeronema moorei*) is found in New Caledonia.

Identification: A herbaceous perennial resembling the *Asphodelus* species. The rhizomes are short and the roots fibrous. The basal leaves are narrow, erect to arching, to lm x 5cm/39 x 2in, tips and margins thickened, carried in tight clumps, glabrous and leathery. The stem leaves are fewer and smaller. The flowering stem is held erect, to 90cm/3ft unbranched, bearing an erect or inclined terminal raceme. The racemes, to 30cm/1ft, are inclined almost horizontally; crowded with short-stalked, red flowers that are held in dense rows along the stem. The perianth segments are bright crimson to deep red, linear, erect. Each flower has six free tepals and six free stamens with persistent filaments. The fruit is purplish, with numerous black seeds.

Distribution: New Zealand (Poor Knights Islands).
Height and spread: lm/39in.
Habit and form: Perennial herb.
Leaf shape: Linear.
Pollinated: Uncertain, insect or bird.

Perching Lily

Kowharawhara, *Astelia solandri*

Distribution: New Zealand.
Height and spread:
1–2m/39–78in.
Habit and form: Herbaceous perennial (usually epiphytic).
Leaf shape: Linear.
Pollinated: Insect.

This grass-like plant, known locally as Kowharawhara, is found in the wet lowland forests of New Zealand, where it is usually epiphytic on tall trees but will also grow on the ground. The sweetly scented flowers appear in January and February on branched panicles and are followed about one year later by distinctive, translucent, green to yellowish fruits. Birds eat the fruit and disperse the seeds.

Identification: An evergreen perennial herb that is usually epiphytic. The rhizomes are short and thick. The leaves are linear, crowded at the base of the stem and 1–2m/39–78in long, to 3.5cm/1⅜in wide, with a spreading, recurved habit. They are glabrous above, three-veined, with a pronounced midrib and covered with chaffy or silky hairs or scales particularly beneath, sometimes so densely as to form a solid covering, amplexicaul. The panicles are few-branched and many-flowered, on stalks 30–100cm/12–39in long, held in leaf rosette, nodding in fruit. The flowers are 15mm/⅝in long, crowded with six lemon-yellow tepals. They can be thin-textured or fleshy, spreading or reflexed.

OTHER SPECIES OF NOTE

Christmas Bells *Blandfordia punicea*
Found in Tasmania, growing in sandy places and acidic moorland, often on wet sites. The coarse leaves are narrow with rough edges, and the tall flower stem is terminated by a beautiful cluster of bell-shaped, tubular flowers that taper to the base. They are scarlet outside and golden-yellow inside.

Common Fringe Lily *Thysanotus tuberosus*
The common fringe lily is found mostly in the eastern parts of mainland Australia, in a variety of situations, ranging from dry hillsides, heath and open forest to grasslands. The bright purple flowers each have three petals with frilly edges that are produced over a long season. The grass-like leaves die off at flowering time.

Spreading Flax Lily *Dianella revolute*
The spreading flax lily is found in New South Wales and Tasmania, on sandy soils near creeks on heaths and in sparse woodlands. It is a tufted plant with flax-like leaves, suckering to form clumps with bright blue flowers borne on branched stems and followed by bright blue fruits. Similar to *D. tasmanica* but favouring drier sites.

Vanilla Lily *Sowerbaea juncea*
Vanilla lily is a plant with soft, onion-like leaves and an erect flower stem that bears a dense cluster of more than 20 soft lilac flowers. Found on wet or waterlogged soils along the coast from Queensland to Victoria it was formerly plentiful and conspicuous in its spring-flowering season, but is now threatened by development.

Flax Lily

Dianella tasmanica

This evergreen perennial plant, found wild in the cool, moist forests of Tasmania and southeast Australia, has arching, thick, strap-like leaves. It bears tall spikes of clustered, nodding, beautiful, star-shaped, bright blue to purple flowers with prominent yellow anthers during spring and summer. These are followed by glossy, deep blue berries that hang for several weeks on delicate stalks.

Identification: This fibrous-rooted herbaceous perennial has a long slender stem to 1.5m/5ft, which stands erect. It is scarred by leaf sheaths and bears a terminal fan of leaves. The grass-like sessile leaves, to 1.2m/4ft long and 2.5cm/1in wide are held rigid. The margins are armed with small, sharp teeth. The inflorescence is a loosely branched panicle. The regular flowers are pale blue, reflexed when mature. Each has six stamens held in two whorls. The anthers are brown and equal to or shorter than the filaments. The dark blue fruit is a globose or oblong-ovoid berry, to 2cm/¾in, broadly oblong and long lasting.

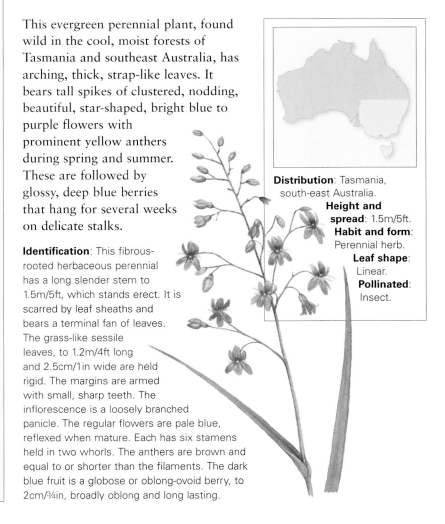

Distribution: Tasmania, south-east Australia.
Height and spread: 1.5m/5ft.
Habit and form: Perennial herb.
Leaf shape: Linear.
Pollinated: Insect.

ORCHIDS

The Orchidaceae, or orchid family, are terrestrial, epiphytic, or saprophytic herbs comprising one of the two largest families of flowering plants. They often display ingenious relationships with their pollinators. The epiphytic types all depend upon the support of another plant and are generally forest dwellers, many living their entire lives on another plant. They include some of the showiest of all flowers.

Banana Orchid

Tiger orchid, *Cymbidium canaliculatum*

This widespread species of orchid is found in the northern parts of western Australia, Northern Territory and north-eastern Queensland down to central New South Wales. It favours the dry inland areas where it shelters in the branch forks and hollow, broken off limbs of large trees in light woodland cover. The deep maroon flowers, have white marks on the lip, and are fragrant, appearing mostly during spring.

Identification: This epiphytic orchid has thick, white branching roots growing from a narrow pseudobulb. The leaves are persistent, glossy, glabrous, to 65cm/26in long, 4cm/1½in wide and stiff. They are olive green, linear, acute, and deeply grooved above. The scapes are arching, crowded, often with several per pseudobulb. Flowers to 4cm/1¾in diameter are variable. The sepals and petals are equal, lanceolate to elliptic, abruptly acute, green, brown or maroon beneath, olive green to pale bronze, streaked or spotted maroon or oxblood above. The lip is ivory, spotted purple or red, minutely pubescent within; midlobe ovate, acute. The callus is pale green or cream, pubescent. The lateral lobes are small, forward-pointing: column half length of lip, thick and incurved.

Distribution: Northern Australia.
Height and spread: 65cm/26in.
Habit and form: Epiphytic orchid.
Leaf shape: Linear.
Pollinated: Insect.

Golden Orchid

Dendrobium discolour

This large tropical epiphytic orchid species, found in Papua New Guinea and Queensland, Australia can commonly be seen perched high up in dead trees of lower altitude rainforests, open forests, mangroves and even on exposed rocky coasts and islets. It often forms extensive colonies, taking root wherever a pocket of soil is available, and its large racemes of flowers are particularly long lasting.

Identification: This erect epiphytic orchid has stems to 5m/16ft tall, to 5cm/2in wide. They are cylindrical, but swollen at the base and in the middle, green or brown in colour, sometimes purple-striped. The leaves, 5–20cm/2–8in long, 2.5–7.5cm/1–3in wide, are elliptical or ovate. The racemes, to 60cm/2ft, are arched and densely flowered. The flowers are cream, yellow, bronze or brown, often flushed with brown or purple. The lip is purple-veined, 2.5cm/1in, trilobed, lateral lobes erect, midlobe recurved, often twisted, ovate. The callus is white with five ridges on the basal half.

Distribution: Papua New Guinea, Australia (Queensland).
Height and spread: To 5m/16ft.
Habit and form: Erect, epiphytic orchid.
Leaf shape: Elliptical.
Pollinated: Insect.

Beard Orchid

Calochilus robertsonii

The beard orchid is aptly named, its lip much resembling a little beard, giving it a unique appearance. It is mostly found on poor soils and in full sun in dry forests, grassy forests, woodlands, heaths and dunes in Tasmania, western Australia, South Australia, Victoria, New South Wales, Queensland and in neighbouring New Zealand. Despite its widespread occurrence, it is never particularly common or abundant where it does occur. The reddish-brown flowers with darker stripes, appear in September to December, opening in succession, resulting in only one open flower per stem at a time.

Identification: A terrestrial orchid, 15–40cm/ 6–16in high when in flower. The solitary leaves are fleshy, linear to lanceolate, thick, forming a v-shape in cross-section, basal, alternate, channelled. Up to six flowers appear on a terminal raceme, each to 2.5cm/1in long, greenish-red with red stripes, appearing in October to December.

Distribution: Australia, New Zealand.
Height and spread: 15–40cm/6–16in.
Habit and form: Terrestrial orchid.
Leaf shape: Linear.
Pollinated: Wasp.

Left: The flowers open in succession with only one per plant at any one time.

OTHER ORCHIDS OF NOTE

Winika *Winika cunninghamii*
This is a sparsely flowered epiphytic orchid that grows mostly high up in the trees in almost full sun in the forests of New Zealand, being endemic to North, South, Stewart and Chatham Islands. It has a special significance to the Maori people as it grew on trees used to make the hull of a sacred war canoe, which they named Te Winika, after the orchid.

Daddy Longlegs
Caladenia filamentosa
Spider orchid
The daddy longlegs or spider orchid is an Australian native found from south-east Queensland to Tasmania, where it occurs in open forests and grassland. A terrestrial orchid, it has a single, narrow, hairy leaf and a basal inflorescence with one to four, greenish-white to reddish or crimson, hairy flowers, appearing from July to October.

Purple Enamel Orchid *Elythranthera brunonis*
Known as purple enamel orchid on account of its large flowers with glossy petals, looking somewhat look like porcelain, this orchid grows fairly commonly on sandy soils north of Perth and east toward Esperance. The solitary leaf appears at the base of the stem and the flowers appear in late summer and midwinter with one to three flowers on an erect scape.

Corybas rivularis

This tiny, but fascinating, orchid bears a solitary, heart-shaped, leaf which lies flat on the ground and produces a stalkless, single, large flower. Endemic to New Zealand throughout the North, South, Stewart, and Auckland Islands, it is mostly found growing within damp, wooded ravines from sea level to 600m/2,000ft. It bears small, pink flowers with long, filamentous tips to the petals and lateral sepals that give it a very characteristic appearance.

Distribution: New Zealand.
Height and spread: 6cm/2¼in.
Habit and form: Terrestrial orchid.
Leaf shape: Ovate.
Pollinated: Insect.

Identification: A terrestrial orchid to 6cm/2¼in high when in flower. The solitary leaf is up to 4cm/1½in long and 2cm/¾in broad. It is ovate-acuminate in shape, cordate at the base, light green above, silvery below, with conspicuous reddish veining. Leaves of young plants are reniform or broadly cordate, without the reddish veining. The usually solitary flower is more or less translucent, with dull red striae. The dorsal sepal is up to 4cm/1½in long. Lateral sepals are filiform, erect and very long, exceeding the flower by as much as 6cm/2¼in. The petals are similar, smaller, horizontal or deflexed. The very short column is hidden in the flower and has a large basal callus.

Peka-a-waka

Hanging tree orchid, *Earina mucronata*

This robust epiphytic species is the most common of New Zealand's perching orchids. It is found on trees in many lowland forests, or in open bush beside tracks, where it grows in huge grassy-looking mats, covering well-lit branches and trunks. The flower stems carry many tiny, yellow-and-orange, sometimes slightly fragrant, flowers in drooping clusters between September and early February. These racemes often persist and flower again the following season.

Identification: A robust epiphytic or lithophytic orchid with creeping, branching fibrous rhizomes that form a thick, tangled mass attached to the tree bark. The stems, to 1m/39in long and marked with black spots, are pendulous. The leaves 5–15cm/2–6in long, to 6mm/¼in wide, are linear, grass-like, slender and pointed. The flower panicle, to 10cm/4in long, with several branches, appears in September to January, with many flowers. Racemes often persist into the following season and flower again. The flowers are slightly fragrant, creamy-yellow, less than 1cm/⅜in across, with oval petals and sepals. The labellum is orange, broad and lobed at its base and outer end.

Distribution: New Zealand.
Height and spread: 1m/39in.
Habit and form: Robust, epiphytic or lithophytic orchid.
Leaf shape: Linear.
Pollinated: Insect.

Left: The creeping fibrous rhizomes often form grassy mats of growth in lowland forests.

Below right: The yellow-and-orange flowers are often slightly fragrant.

Hooded Orchid

Pterostylis banksii

This small, widespread and variable species is common throughout New Zealand. It can be found in lowland to montane forests and forest margins as well as scrub. It is distinctive in having flowers equipped with a mobile lip, which is a pollination adaptation. The pollinating insect lands on the flower, and alights on the lip; its weight causes the lip to tip, thereby forcing the insect into a position where it pollinates the flower. It is one of the larger green-hooded orchids having green flowers marked with translucent, white stripes that appear from October until December.

Distribution: New Zealand.
Height and spread: 35cm/14in.
Habit and form: Terrestrial orchid.
Leaf shape: Linear.
Pollinator: Insect.

Identification: A terrestrial deciduous orchid, to 35cm/14in tall, with subterranean, fibrous tubers. The stems are basally sheathed. Each has four to six leaves, to 20cm/8in long, in a basal rosette. They are linear, keeled beneath, pale green, with a paler midrib. The flowers are pale green with darker stripes. The petals and sepals are tipped orange-pink. The lip has a single red ridge above, and green margins. The dorsal sepal is incurved and arched, and has the petals pressed against it, forming a hood and concealing the column.

Far left: The distinctive green, hooded flowers are borne singly on long stems.

Left: The flowers are equipped with a mobile lip that aids in insect pollination.

Varavara

Spathoglottis pacifica

This large terrestrial orchid with rhizomes and pseudobulbs is common along roadsides, forest margins, open forest and open areas, ranging from sea-level to 1,000m/3,250ft in its native Fiji, where it is also widely cultivated as a garden ornamental. Restricted to Fiji, Vanuatu, Wallis Islands and Samoa, the large, showy, pink or mauve flowers are borne profusely on many-flowered racemes, which arise from the base of the pseudobulbs, with flowers and fruit being visible on each plant throughout the year.

Identification: A fibrous-rooted terrestrial orchid, with rhizomes and broad, conical to ovoid, sheathed pseudobulbs. The stem is thin, erect and bears few leaves. The leaves are lanceolate and basally sheathing. The inflorescence is a many-flowered raceme arising from basal leaf axils. The many large flowers are showy, pink or mauve.

Distribution: Fiji, Vanuatu, Wallis Islands, Samoa.
Height and spread: Variable.
Habit and form: Fibrous-rooted, terrestrial orchid.
Leaf shape: Lanceolate.
Pollinated: Insect.

Top left: The showy flowers are large and pink.

Left: This large orchid is terrestrial and often seen by roadsides.

OTHER ORCHIDS OF NOTE

Common Onion Orchid *Microtis unifolia*
This is a variable plant with a single tubular leaf and flower stem. It has 5–40 green flowers emerging from the leaf about a third to half way up the stem. It occurs practically everywhere in New Zealand except for dark forests and is the country's most common orchid species to be seen flowering between November and January.

Dotted Sun Orchid *Thelymitra ixioides*
A relatively small terrestrial orchid species found in scrub and roadsides in scattered localities from the northwest of South Island, New Zealand. It has a single, wide, fleshy, deeply channelled leaf and up to 20 or more flowers, which are blue with darker spots that appear from October to December.

Cowslip Orchid *Caladenia flava*
This orchid has a wide distribution on sandy soils across much of Australia. The flowers appear between September and November. It is variable in flower colour, the yellow flowers sometimes having little or no red colouring, while others are quite streaked and spotted.

Tahitian Vanilla
Vanilla tahitiensis
Tahitian vanilla has large and attractive, cream-coloured flowers with a sweet scent. Its leaves are thick and leathery, and it is occasionally grown for its pods, which when dried, become an alternative source of the spice vanilla.

Nodding Greenhood

Pterostylis nutans

This terrestrial orchid, widespread in all states except western Australia and the Northern Territory, also occurs as a small, vagrant population on New Zealand's North Island. It can be found from sea level to almost 1,000m/3,300ft in light scrub and is a distinctive species because of its drooping, hooded flowers occurring singly during the winter and spring.

Identification: A deciduous orchid to 30cm/1ft tall with subterranean tubers. It has three to six ovate to oblong leaves held in a basal rosette to 3cm/1¼in long and 2cm/¾in wide. Each has one or two translucent, green striped flowers, sometimes tipped red, with the dorsal sepal incurved and arched, forming a hood that conceals the column. The lateral sepals loosely embrace the hood, and are fused into a lower lip. The lip has a mobile claw and often a basal appendage. It is sharply recurved, to 15mm/⅝in, green in colour with a central red-brown ridge.

Distribution: Australia, New Zealand.
Height and spread: 30cm/1ft.
Habit and form: Terrestrial orchid.
Leaf shape: Ovate to oblong.
Pollinated: Insect.

Right: The sepal and petals combine to form a hood.

Left: The plant is noticeable in winter and spring.

GLOSSARY

Annual a plant which completes its entire life-cycle within a year.

Anther the pollen-bearing portion of the stamen.

Areole elevation on a cactus stem, bearing a spine.

Axil the upper angle between an axis and any off-shoot or lateral organ arising from it, especially a leaf.

Axillary situated in, or arising from, or pertaining to an axil.

Basal leaf arising from the rootstock or a very short or buried stem.

Beak a long, pointed, horn-like projection; particularly applied to the terminal points of fruits and pistils.

Beaked furnished with a beak.

Beard (on flower) a tuft or zone of hair as on the falls of bearded irises.

Berry indehiscent (non-drying) fruit, one- to many-seeded; the product of a single pistil. Frequently misapplied to any pulpy or fleshy fruit regardless of its constitution.

Biennial lasting for two seasons from germination to death, generally blooming in the second season.

Boss-like (of the standard) Taking on the appearance of a boss (round metal stud in the centre of a shield or ornamental work).

Bract a modified protective leaf associated with the inflorescence (clothing the stalk and subtending the flowers), with buds and with newly emerging shoots.

Branched rootstock a branching underground stem.

Bromeliad a type of South American plant predominantly found growing on other plants but not parasitically.

Calcicole a plant dwelling on and favouring calcareous (lime-rich) soils.

Calcifuge a plant avoiding and damaged by calcareous soils.

Callus ridge (calli) superficial protuberances on the lip of many orchid flowers.

Capsule (of fruit) a dry (dehiscent) seed vessel.

Carpet-forming with a dense, ground-hugging habit; hence "carpet-like".

Cauline (of leaves) attached to or arising from the stem.

Chlorophyll green pigment that facilitates food production, is present in most plants.

Cleistogamous with self-pollination occurring in the closed flower.

Climbing habit any plant that climbs or has a tendency to do so, usually by means of various adaptations of stems, leaves or roots.

Clubbed spur a tubular or sac-like basal extension of a flower, generally projecting backward and containing nectar, gradually thickening upward from a slender base.

Clump-forming forming a tight mass of close-growing stems or leaves at or near ground level.

Column (of the flower) a feature of orchids, where the style and stamens are fused together in a single structure.

Composite (of flowers and leaves) a single leaf or petal divided in such a way as to resemble many.

Compound (of flowers and leaves) divided into two or more subsidiary parts.

Contractile roots roots which contract in length and pull parts of a plant further into the soil.

Convex petal with an outline or shape like that of the exterior of a sphere.

Cordate heart-shaped.

Cormous perennial a plant or stem base living for two or more years with a solid, swollen, subterranean, bulb-like stem.

Corolla a floral envelope composed of free or fused petals.

Corona a crown or cup-like appendage or ring of appendages.

Corymb an indeterminate flat-topped or convex inflorescence, where the outer flowers open first.

Creeping habit trailing on or under the

surface, and sometimes rooting.

Culms the stems of grasses.

Cupped (flowers) shaped like a cup.

Curving spur a tubular or sac-like basal extension of a flower, generally projecting backward and containing nectar, being curved in shape.

Cyathia flower form, shaped like a cup.

Cylindrical follicle cylindrical elongated fruit, virtually circular in cross-section.

Cyme (flowers) a more or less flat-topped and determinate flowerhead, with the central or terminal flower opening first.

Decumbent base (of the stem) lying horizontally along the ground but with the apex ascending and almost erect.

Decurrent where the base of a leaf extends down to the petiole (if any) and the stem.

Deeply cut petals or leaves with deeply incised lobes.

Deeply segmented petals or leaves that are sharply divided into several segments.

Deltoid an equilateral triangle attached by the broad end rather than the point; shaped like the Greek letter delta.

Dilated concavity dilating, broadened, expanded, in the manner of the outer surface of a sphere.

Dioecious with male and female flowers on different plants.

Disc floret part of the central flowerhead in the Asteraceae. Short tubular florets as opposed to the peripheral ray florets.

Dissected leaf shape cut in any way; a term applicable to leaf blades or other flattened organs that are incised.

Domed flowerhead Compound flowerhead arranged in a dome shape.

Drupe a one- to several-seeded fruit, contained within a soft, fleshy pericarp, as in stone fruits.

Ellipsoid resembling an ellipse shape.
Epidermis the outer layer of plant tissue; skin.
Epiphytic growing on plants without being parasitic.
Ericaceous in broad terms, resembling *Erica* spp. In habit, plants preferring acidic soil conditions.
Evergreen plant with foliage that remains green for at least a year, through more than one growing season.

Farinose having a mealy, granular texture on the surface.
Filament stalk that bears the anther at its tips, together forming a stamen.
Floret a very small flower, generally part of a congested inflorescence.

Genus The first name of a plant described under the binomial system of botanical naming.
Glandular bearing glands, or hairs with gland-like prominence at the tip.
Glandular inflorescence a compound flowerhead with a glandular surface.
Glycoside A compound related to sugar that plays many important roles in living organisms, with numerous plant-produced glycosides used as medications.

Hastate arrow-shaped, triangular, with two equal and approximately triangular basal lobes, pointing laterally outward rather than toward the stalk.
Haustorium a sucker in parasitic plants that penetrates the host.
Hemi-parasite only parasitic for part of its life cycle; not entirely dependent upon the host for nutrition.
Hemispheric a half sphere shape.
Herb abbreviation for herbaceous. Not the culinary herb.
Herbaceous pertaining to herbs, i.e. lacking persistent aerial parts or lacking woody parts.
Herbaceous perennial herbaceous plant living for three or more years. Referred to as herb.
Hip the fleshy, developed floral cup and the enclosed seeds of a rose.
Hooded flowers one or more petals, fused and forming a hood over the sexual reproductive parts of the flower.
Hooked spurs a tubular or sac-like basal extension of a flower, generally projecting backwards and containing nectar; being hooked in shape.

Inflorescences the arrangement of flowers and their accessory parts in multiple heads, on a central axis or stem.

Keeled (leaves) a prominent ridge, like the keel of a boat, running longitudinally down the centre of the undersurface of a leaf.

Labellum a lip, especially the enlarged or otherwise distinctive third petal of an orchid.
Layering stems rooting on contact with the earth and forming colonies of cloned plants.
Leaf
  Lobed divided into (usually rounded) segments, lobes, separated from adjacent segments.
  Toothed possessing teeth, often qualified, as saw-toothed or bluntly toothed.
  Uneven margins with one margin exceeding the one opposite.
  Wavy margin having a wavy edge.
Leaf axil the point immediately above the point of leaf attachment, often containing a bud.
Leaf tip
  pointed ending in a distinct point.
  rounded with no visible point.
Leaflet units of a compound leaf.
Lenticel elliptical and raised cellular pore on the surface of bark or the surface tissue of fruit, through which gases can penetrate.

Liana a woody climbing vine.
Lignotuber a starchy swelling on underground stems or roots, often used to survive fire or browsing animals.
Lip petal, or part thereof, which is either modified or differentiated from the others, on which insects can alight.
Lithophytic growing on rocks or stony soil, deriving nourishment from the atmosphere rather than the soil.
Low-growing plants that do not reach any significant height; ground hugging.

Membranous capsule seedpod with thin walls.
Mesic a type of habitat with a moderate or well-balanced supply of moisture, e.g. a mesic forest.
Midrib the primary vein of a leaf or leaflet, usually running down its centre as a continuation of the leaf stem.
Monocarpic dying after flowering and bearing fruit only once.
Monopedal a stem or rhizome in which growth continues indefinitely from the apical or terminal bud, and generally exhibits no secondary branching.
Monoecious A plant with both male and female flowers/flower parts on the same plant (syn. Hermaphrodite).
Morphologically pertaining to the study of the form of plants.
Mucilage viscous substance obtained from plant seeds exposed to water.

Nectary a gland, often in the form of a protuberance or depression, which secretes and sometimes absorbs nectar.
Node the point on a stem where one or more leaves, shoots, whorls, branches or flowers are attached.

Open habit growing loosely with space between the branches.

Panicle indeterminate branched inflorescence, the branches generally resemble racemes or corymbs.

Pea-like flowers that are like those of the pea (*Psium* spp.).

Pendent hanging downward, more markedly than arching or nodding but not as a result of the weight of the part in question or the weakness of its attachment or support.

Pendent raceme raceme inflorescence with a pendent habit.

Pendulous branch branch with a pendent habit.

Perennial a plant lasting for three seasons or more.

Perfoliate a sessile leaf of which the basal lobes are united, the stem seems to pass through the blade.

Perianth the collective term for the floral envelopes, the corolla and calyx, especially when the two are not clearly differentiated.

Perianth tube the effect of fused petals resulting in a tubular flower shape

Petaloid sepal segment that encloses the flower when in bud that resembles a true petal.

Petaloid tepal tepal that resembles a petal.

Photosynthesis the synthesis of sugar and oxygen from carbon dioxide and water, carried out by all green plants.

Pinnate feather-like; an arrangement of more than three leaflets in two rows.

Pinnatifid pinnately cleft nearly to the midrib in broad divisions, but without separating into distinct leaflets or pinnae.

Pistil the female reproductive organs of a flower consisting of one or more carpel.

Pod appendage containing seeds:
  Inflated pod fruits that are inflated and balloon like
  Cylindrical pod elongated fruits, virtually circular in cross-section.
  Flattened pod distinctly flattened along one plane.

Pinnatisect shape deeply and pinnately cut to, or near to, the midrib; the divisions, narrower than in pinnatifid, are not truly distinct segments.

Pouched bracts a modified protective leaf associated with the inflorescence and possessing a pouched shape.

Primary rays The outer petaloid rays, usually associated with a composite flower such as those in Asteraceae.

Procumbent trailing loosely or lying flat along the surface of the ground, without rooting.

Prostate lying flat on the ground.

Pseudobulb the water-storing thickened "bulb-like" stem found in many sympodial orchids.

Pseudostem not a true stem but made up of leaf sheaths.

Quadrangular stem four-angled, as in the stems of some *Passiflora* and succulent *Euphorbia* spp.

Raceme an indeterminate, un-branched and elongate inflorescence composed of flowers in stalks.

Ramicaul thin leaf stem usually associated with orchids.

Rambling habit an unruly spreading or partially climbing growth habit.

Ray floret a small flower with a tubular corolla and the limb expanded and flattened in a strap-like blade, usually occupying the outer rings of a capitulum (daisy flower).

Reflexed abruptly deflexed at more than a 90 degree angle.

Reniform kidney shaped.

Reniform scale kidney-shaped leaf scale.

Rhizome underground stem.

Rhizomatous producing or possessing rhizomes; rhizome-like.

Rhombic ovate oval to diamond-shaped; angularly oval, the base and apex forming acute angles.

Root sucker stem arising directly from the roots of a parent plant.

Rootstock the roots and stem base of a plant.

Rosette forming leaves arranged in a basal rosette or rosettes.

Runcinate a leaf, petal or petal-like structure, usually oblanceolate in outline and with sharp, prominent teeth or broad, incised lobes pointing backward toward the base, away from a generally acute apex, as in *Taraxacum* (dandelion).

Runner prostrate or recumbent stem, taking root and giving rise to a plantlet at its apex and sometimes at nodes.

Sagittate arrow- or spear-shaped, where the equal and approximately triangular basal lobes of leaves point downward or toward the stalk.

Saprophytic deriving its nutrition from dissolved or decayed organic matter.

Scalloped rounded in outline in the manner of a scallop shell.

Scape an erect, leafless stalk, supporting an inflorescence or flower.

Scrambling habit not strictly climbing but vigorous with a tendency to grow over surrounding vegetation.

Seed ripened, fertilized ovule; an embryonic plant.

Seedhead describes the fruiting bodies of a plant.

Seedpod describes the enclosing body around developing seeds.

Semipendent flowerhead only partially pendent in nature.

Sepal modified leaf-like structure, enclosing and protecting the inner floral parts prior to its opening.

Serrated toothed margin, with teeth resembling those of a saw.

Shrub a loose descriptive term for a woody plant which produces multiple stems, shoots or branches from its base, but does not have a single trunk.

Shrublet a small shrub or a dwarf, woody-based and closely branched plant.

Sickle-shaped crescent-shaped.

Single flowers with one set of petals.

Solitary flowers borne singly (i.e. not in an inflorescence).

Spadix (Spadisces pl.) a fleshy, columnar flower, often enclosed in a spathe and typical of plants in the family Araceae.

Spathe a conspicuous leaf or bract subtending a spadix or other inflorescence.

Spathulate spatula-shaped, essentially oblong, but attenuated at the base and rounded at the apex.

Species the second name used to identify a plant with particular characteristics under the binomial system of botanical naming.

Spike an indeterminate inflorescence bearing sessile flowers on an un-branched axis.

Sprawling spreading in an untidy manner.

Spreading stems or branches extending horizontally outward.

Spur a tubular or sac-like basal extension of the flower, projecting backward and often containing nectar.

Stalked a general term for the stem-like support of any organ.

Stamen the male floral organ, bearing an anther, generally on a filament, and producing pollen.

Staminode sterile stamen or stamen-like structure, often rudimentary or modified, sometimes petal-like and frequently antherless.

Standard (1) in pea flowers, the large, uppermost petal; (2) an erect or ascending unit of the inner whorl of an *Iris* flower.

Stigma the end of a pistil that receives the pollen and normally differs in

texture from the rest of the style.

Stipule leafy or bract-like appendage at the base of a leaf stem, usually occurring in pairs and soon shed.

Stolon a prostrate or recumbent stem, taking root and giving rise to plantlets at its apex and sometimes at nodes.

Stoloniferous possessing stolons.

Straggly untidy, rather stretched in appearance.

Subopposite more or less opposite, but with one leaf or leaflet of a pair slightly above or below its partner.

Suborbicular more or less circular.

Subshrub a perennial with a woody base and soft shoots.

Subspecies a species further divided into distinct populations.

Succulent thickly cellular and fleshy.

Suckering shrub shrub with a tendency to produce root suckers as part of its normal growth.

Tendril a modified branch, leaf or axis, filiform, scandent, and capable of attaching itself to a support either by twining or adhesion.

Tepal perianth segment that cannot be defined as either petal or sepal.

Terminal at the tip or apex of a stem.

Terrestrial living on land; growing in the soil.

Tessellated chequered, composed of small squares as in the flower of *Fritillaria meleagris* or the intersecting vein pattern of some leaves.

Thorn sharp hard outgrowth from the stem wood.

Throat the central opening of tubular or bell-shaped flowers.

Toothed margin leaf edge possessing teeth, often qualified, as saw-toothed or bluntly toothed.

Trailing prostrate but not rooting.

Trefoil leaf divided into three leaflets.

Trifoliate three-leaved.

Tuberoid in the manner of a tuber.

Tuberous bearing tubers, tuberous-bearing tubers, or resembling a tuber.

Tulip-shaped similar shape to the flower of a tulip.

Tussock-forming forming a tight mass of close growing stems or leaves at or near ground level, with grass-like leaves.

Twining vine a climbing plant that twines around a support.

Two-lipped (flower) with two lips.

Umbellate pattern resembling an umbel.

Umbel a flat-topped inflorescence like a corymb, but with all the flowered pedicels (rays) arising from the same point at the apex of the main axis.

Unisexual a flower that is either male or female.

Upright a flowerhead that is held vertically or nearly so.

Upright habit Growth that is vertical or nearly so.

Variety a distinct population that does not merit the status of species or sub-species in its own right.

Vein/veinlets an externally visible strand of vascular tissue.

Vestigial a leaf that was functional and fully developed in ancestral forms, but is now smaller and less developed.

Vine a general term to describe some climbing plants.

Whorl when three or more organs are arranged in a circle at one node or, loosely, around the same axis.

Woody ligneous (containing the plant protein lignin), approaching the nature of wood.

Acknowledgments

With thanks to Spillifords Wildlife Garden, Devon, and The English Cottage Garden Nursery, Kent. The publishers would like to thank the following people and picture libraries for permission to use their images: Ardea page 28 br, page 29tc, 32. DW Stock Picture Library page 171, 64, 74b, 84, 90b, 98. Natural Science Image Library page 75, 80, 90t, 95, 102. OSF page 108. Peter Barrett page 24bc. Photos Horticultural page 28bl, 68, 74t, 78.

INDEX

t = top, b= bottom, l= left, r= right

P122t Callistemon sp; b Alyogyne huegelii. P123t Anigosanthos manglesii; b Dyrandra polycephala. P124t Lepospermum myrsinoides; b Epacris longiflorum. P125t Isopogon anemonifolius; b Hardenbergia comtoniana. P126tl lyogyne huegelii; tr Pycnosorus globosus; bl Telopea oreades; br Scaevola aemula. P127tl Xerochrysum bracteatum; tr Hakea mitchelli; bl Banksia marginata; br Grevillea sp. P128tl Diplarrhena morea; tr Pultenaea sp; bl Acacia brachybotrya; br Correa reflexa.